A Short Account of the

Destruction of the Indies

Or, a faithful NARRATIVE OF THE Horrid and
Unexampled Massacres, Butcheries, and all manner of
Cruelties, ... the time of its first Discovery by them.

By Bartolomé de las Casas

Published by Pantianos Classics

ISBN-13: 978-1539797722

First published in 1552

Contents

Popery Truly Display'd in its Bloody Colours:

OR,

A faithful Narrative of the Horrid and Unexampled Massacres, Butcheries, and all manner of Cruelties, that Hell and Malice could invent, committed by the Popish Spanish Party on the inhabitants of West-India.

TOGETHER

With the Devastations of several Kingdoms in America by Fire and Sword, for the space of Forty and Two Years, from the time of its first Discovery by them.

Composed first in Spanish by Bartholomew de las Casas, a Bishop there, and Eye-Witness of most of these Barbarous Cruelties; afterward Translated by him into Latin, then by other hands, into High-Dutch, Low-Dutch, French, and now Taught to Speak Modern English. London, Printed for R. Hewson at the Crown in Cornhil, near the Stocks-Market. 1689.

The Argument of This Narrative By way of Preface to the Reader

The Reverend Author of this Compendious Summary was Bartholomaeus de las Casas alias Casaus, a Pious and Religeous person, (as appears by his zealous Transports in this Narrative for promotion of the Christian Faith) elevated from a Frier of the Dominican Order to sit in the Episcopal Chair, who was frequently importuned by Good and Learned Men, particularly Historians, to Publish this Summary, who so prevailed with him, that he Collected out of that copious History which might and ought to be written on this subject, the contents of this concise Treatise with intention to display unto the World the Enormities, &c. the Spaniards committed in America during their residence there, to their eternal ignominy; and for the author finding that no Admonitions or Reprehensions, how mild soever could operate upon or sink into the rocky-hearted Tyrants in those Occidental parts; he therefore took up a firm resolution, being then about 50 years of age (as he himself declares) to run the Hazards and Dangers by Sea, and the Risque of a long voyage into Spain there to acquaint and Certifie the most Illustrious Prince Phillip the Son and Heir of his Imperial Majesty Charles the Fifth of Blessed Memory, with the Horrid crimes, &c. perpetrated in those countries, part whereof he had seen, and part heard from such as boasted of their Wickedness. Whereupon his Caeserean Majesty moved with a tender and Christian compassion towards these Inhabitants of the Countries of America, languishing for want of redress, he called a Council at Valedolid, Anno Dom. 1542. consisting of Learned and Able Men, in order to the reformation of the West-Indian government, and took such a course, that from that time their Tyranny and cruelty against those Barbarians was somewhat repressed, and those Nations in some measure delivered from that intolerable and more then Aegyptian Bondage, or at least the Spaniards ill usage and treatment of the Americans was alleviated and abated. This Book mostly Historical, part Typographical, was Published first by the Author in Spanish at Sevil, after that

Translated into Latin by himself; and in process of time into High Dutch, Low Dutch, French and now English; which is the Sixth Language it has been taught to speak, that anyone of what Nation soever might in this Narrative contemplate and see as in a mirror the dismal and pernitious fruits, that lacquey and attend unlimited and close fisted Avarice, and thereby Learn to abhor and detest it, Cane pejus & angue: it being the predominant and chiefest motive to the comission of such inexpressible Outrages, as here in part are faintly, not fully represented. Which sin the Pagan Indians themselves did exprobate in the Spaniards with all Detestation, Ignominy and Disgrace: for when they had taken some of them Prisoners (which was rarely) they bound them hand and foot, laid them on the ground, and then pouring melted Gold down their Throats, cried out and called to them aloud in derision, yield, throw up thy Gold O Christian! Vomit and spew out the Mettal which hath so inqinated and invenom'd both Body and Soul, that hath stain'd and infected they mind with desires and contrivances, and thy hands with Commission of such matchless Enormities. I will then shut up all this, being but an Extract of what is in the Prefatory part of the Original. I earnestly beg and desire all Men to be perswaded, that this summary was not published upon any private Design, sinister ends or affection in favor or prejudice of any particular Nation; but for the publick Emolument and Advantage of all true Christians and moral Men throughout the whole World.

Farewell

The Cruelties of the Spaniards Committed in America

America was discovered and found out Ann. Dom. 1492, and the Year insuing inhabited by the Spaniards, and afterward a multitude of them travelled thither from Spain for the space of Nine and Forty Years. Their first attempt was on the Spanish Island, which indeed is a most fertile soil, and at present in great reputation for its Spaciousness and Length, containing in Circumference Six Hundred Miles: Nay it is on all sides surrounded with an almost innumerable number of Islands, which we found so well peopled with Natives and Forreigners, that there is scarce any Region in the Universe fortified with so many Inhabitants: But the main Land or Continent, distant from this Island Two Hundred and Fifty Miles and upwards, extends it self above Ten Thousand Miles in Length near the sea-shore, which Lands are some of them already discover'd, and more may be found out in process of time: And such a multitude of People inhabits these Countries, that it seems as if the Omnipotent God has Assembled and Convocated the major part of Mankind in this part of the World.

Now this infinite multitude of Men are by the Creation of God innocently simple, altogether void of and averse to all manner of Craft, Subtlety and Malice, and most Obedient and Loyal Subjects to their Native Sovereigns; and behave themselves very patiently, sumissively and quietly towards the Spaniards, to whom they are subservient and subject; so that finally they live without the least thirst after revenge, laying aside all litigiousness, Commotion and hatred.

This is a most tender and effeminate people, and so imbecile and unequal-balanced temper, that they are altogether incapable of hard labour, and in few years, by one Distemper or other soon expire, so

7

that the very issue of Lords and Princes, who among us live with great affluence, and fard deliciously, are not more effminate and tender than the Children of their Husbandmen or Labourers: This Nation is very Necessitous and Indigent, Masters of very slender Possessions, and consequently, neither Haughty, nor Ambitious. They are parsimonious in their Diet, as the Holy Fathers were in their frugal life in the Desert, known by the name of Eremites. They go naked, having no other Covering but what conceals their Pudends from publick sight. An hairy Plad, or loose Coat, about an Ell, or a coarse woven Cloth at most Two Ells long serves them for the warmest Winter Garment. They lye on a coarse Rug or Matt, and those that have the most plentiful Estate or Fortunes, the better sort, use Net-work, knotted at the four corners in lieu of Beds, which the Inhabitants of the Island of Hispaniola, in their own proper Idiom, term Hammacks. The Men are pregnant and docible. The natives tractable, and capable of Morality or Goodness, very apt to receive the instill'd principles of Catholick Religion; nor are they averse to Civility and good Manners, being not so much discompos'd by variety of Obstructions, as the rest of Mankind; insomuch, that having suckt in (if I may so express my self) the the very first Rudiments of the Christian Faith, they are so transported with Zeal and Furvor in the exercise of Ecclesiastical Sacraments, and Divine Service, that the very Religioso's themselves, stand in need of the greatest and most signal patience to undergo such extream Transports. And to conclude, I my self have heard the Spaniards themselves (who dare not assume the Confidence to deny the good Nature praedominant in them) declare, that there was nothing wanting in them for the acquisition of Eternal Beatitude, but the sole Knowledge and Understanding of the Deity.

The Spaniards first assaulted the innocent Sheep, so qualified by the Almighty, as is premention'd, like most cruel Tygers, Wolves and Lions hunger-starv'd, studying nothing, for the space of Forty Years, after their first landing, but the Massacre of these Wretches, whom they have so inhumanely and barbarously butcher'd and harass'd with several kinds of Torments, never before known, or heard (of which you shall have some account in the following Discourse) that of Three Millions of Persons, which lived in Hispaniola itself, there is at present but the inconsiderable remnant of scarce Three Hundred. Nay the Isle of Cuba, which extends as far, as Valledolid in Spain is distant from Rome, lies now uncultivated, like a Desert, and intomb'd in its own Ruins. You may also find the Isles of St. John, and Jamaica, both large and fruitful places, unpeopled and desolate. The Lucayan Islands on the North Side, adjacent to Hispaniola and Cuba, which are Sixty in number, or thereabout, together with with those, vulgarly known by the name of the Gigantic Isles, and others, the most infertile whereof, exceeds the Royal Garden of Sevil in fruitfulness, a most Healthful and pleasant Climat, is now laid waste and uninhabited; and whereas, when the Spaniards first arriv'd here, about Five Hundred Thousand Men dwelt in it, they are now cut off, some by slaughter, and others ravished away by Force and Violence, to work in the Mines of Hispanioloa, which was destitute of Native Inhabitants: For a certain Vessel, sailing to this Isle, to the end, that the Harvest being over (some good Christian, moved with Piety and Pity, undertook this dangerous Voyage, to convert Souls to Christianity) the remaining gleanings might be gathered up, there were only found Eleven Persons, which I saw with my own Eyes. There are other Islands Thirty in number, and upward bordering upon the Isle of St. John, totally unpeopled; all which are above Two Thousand miles in Lenght, and yet remain without Inhabitants, Native, or People.

As to the firm land, we are certainly satisfied, and assur'd, that the Spaniards by their barbarous and execrable Actions have absolutely depopulated Ten Kingdoms, of greater extent than all Spain, together with the Kingdoms of Arragon and Portugal, that is to say, above One Thousand Miles, which now lye wast and desolate, and are absolutely ruined, when as formerly no other Country whatsoever was more populous. Nay we dare boldly affirm, that during the Forty Years space, wherein they exercised their sanguinary and detestable Tyranny in these Regions, above Twelve Millions (computing Men, Women, and Children) have undeservedly perished; nor do I conceive that I should deviate from the Truth by saying that above Fifty Millions in all paid their last Debt to Nature.

Those that arriv'd at these Islands from the remotest parts of Spain, and who pride themselves in the Name of Christians, steer'd Two courses principally, in order to the Extirpation, and Exterminating of this People from the face of the Earth. The first whereof was raising an unjust, sanguinolent, cruel War. The other, by putting them to death, who hitherto, thirsted after their Liberty, or design'd (which the most Potent, Strenuous and Magnanimous Spirits intended) to recover their pristin Freedom, and shake off the Shackles of so injurious a Captivity: For they being taken off in War, none but Women and Children were permitted to enjoy the benefit of that Country-Air, in whom they did in succeeding times lay such a heavy Yoak, that the very Brutes were more happy than they: To which Two Species of Tyranny as subalternate things to the Genus, the other innumerable Courses they took to extirpate and make this a desolate People, may be reduced and referr'd.

Now the ultimate end and scope that incited the Spaniards to endeavor the Extirptaion and Desolation of this People, was Gold only; that thereby growing opulent in a short time, they might arrive at once at such Degrees and Dignities, as were no wayes consistent with their Persons.

Finally, in one word, their Ambition and Avarice, than which the heart of Man never entertained greater, and the vast Wealth of those Regions; the Humility and Patience of the Inhabitants (which made their approach to these Lands more facil and easie) did much promote the business: Whom they so despicably contemned, that they treated them (I speak of things which I was an Eye Witness of, without the least fallacy) not as Beasts, which I cordially wished they would, but as the most abject dung and filth of the Earth; and so sollicitous they were of their Life and Soul, that the above-mentioned number of People died without understanding the true Faith or Sacraments. And this also is as really true as the praecendent Narration (which the very Tyrants and cruel Murderers cannot deny without the stigma of a lye) that the Spaniards never received any injury from the Indians, but that they rather reverenced them as Persons descended from Heaven, until that they were compelled to take up Arms, provoked thereunto by repeated Injuries, violent Torments, and injust Butcheries.

Of the Island Hispaniola

In this Isle, which, as we have said, the Spaniards first attempted, the bloody slaughter and destruction of Men first began: for they violently forced away Women and Children to make them Slaves, and ill-treated them, consuming and wasting their Food, which they had purchased with great sweat, toil, and yet remained dissatisfied too, which every one according to his strength and ability, and that was very inconsiderable (for they provided no other Food than what was absolutely necessary to support Nature without superfluity, freely bestow'd on them, and one individual Spaniard consumed more Victuals in one day, than would serve to maintain Three Families a Month, every one consisting of Ten Persons. Now being oppressed by such evil usage, and afflicted with such greate Torments and violent Entertainment they began to understand that such Men as those had not their Mission from Heaven; and therefore some of them conceal'd their Provisions and others to their Wives and Children in lurking holes, but some, to avoid the obdurate and dreadful temper of such a Nation, sought their Refuge on the craggy tops of Mountains; for the Spaniards did not only entertain them with Cuffs, Blows, and wicked Cudgelling, but laid violent hands also on the Governours of Cities; and this arriv'd at length to that height of Temerity and Impudence, that a certain Captain was so audacious as abuse the Consort of the most puissant King of the whole Isle. From which time they began to consider by what wayes and means they might expel the Spaniards out of their Countrey, and immediately took up Arms. But, good God, what Arms, do you imagin? Namely such, both Offensive and Defensive, as resemble

Reeds wherewith Boys sport with one another, more than Manly Arms and Weapons.

Which the Spaniards no sooner perceived, but they, mounted on generous Steeds, well weapon'd with Lances and Swords, begin to exercise their bloody Butcheries and Strategems, and overrunning their Cities and Towns, spar'd no Age, or Sex, nay not so much as Women with Child, but ripping up their Bellies, tore them alive in pieces. They laid Wagers among themselves, who should with a Sword at one blow cut, or divide a Man in two; or which of them should decollate or behead a Man, with the greatest dexterity; nay farther, which should sheath his Sword in the Bowels of a Man with the quickest dispatch and expedition.

They snatcht young Babes from the Mothers Breasts, and then dasht out the brains of those innocents against the Rocks; others they cast into Rivers scoffing and jeering them, and call'd upon their Bodies when falling with derision, the true testimony of their Cruelty, to come to them, and inhumanely exposing others to their Merciless Swords, together with the Mothers that gave them Life.

They erected certain Gibbets, large, but low made, so that their feet almost reacht the ground, every one of which was so order'd as to bear Thirteen Persons in Honour and Reverence (as they said blasphemously) of our Redeemer and his Twelve Apostles, under which they made a Fire to burn them to Ashes whilst hanging on them: But those they intended to preserve alive, they dismiss'd, their Hands half cut, and still hanging by the Skin, to carry their Letters missive to those that fly from us and ly sculking on the Mountains, as an exprobation of their flight.

The Lords and Persons of Noble Extract were usually expos'd to this kind of Death; they order'd Gridirons to be placed and supported with wooden Forks, and putting a small Fire under them, these miserable Wretches by degrees and with loud Shreiks and exquisite Torments, at last Expir'd.

I once saw Four or Five of their most Powerful Lords laid on these Gridirons, and thereon roasted, and not far off, Two or Three more over-spread with the same Commodity, Man's Flesh; but the shril Clamours which were heard there being offensive to the Captain, by hindring his Repose, he commanded them to be strangled with a Halter. The Executioner (whose Name and Parents at Sevil are not unknown to me) prohibited the doing of it; but stopt Gags into their Mouths to prevent the hearing of the noise (he himself making the Fire) till that they dyed, when they had been roasted as long as he thought convenient. I was an Eye-Witness of these and and innumerable Number of other Cruelties: And because all Men, who could lay hold of the opportunity, sought out lurking holes in the Mountains, to avoid as dangerous Rocks so Brutish and Barbarous a People, Strangers to all Goodness, and the Extirpaters and Adversaries of Men, they bred up such fierce hunting Dogs as would devour an Indian like a Hog, at first sight in less than a moment: Now such kind of Slaughters and Cruelties as these were committed by the Curs, and if at any time it hapned, (which was rarely) that the Indians irritated upon a just account destroy'd or took away the Life of any Spaniard, they promulgated and proclaim'd this Law among them, that One Hundred Indians should dye for every individual Spaniard that should be slain.

Of the Kingdoms contained in Hispaniola

This Isle of Hispaniola was made up of Six of their greatest Kingdoms, and as many most Puissant Kings, to whose Empire almost all the other Lords, whose Number was infinite, did pay their Allegiance. One of these Kingdoms was called Magua, signifying a Campaign or open Country; which is very observable, if any place in the Universe deserves taking notice of, and memorable for the pleasantness of its Situation; for it is extended from South to North Eighty Miles, in breadth Five, Eight, and in some parts Ten Miles in length; and is on all sides inclosed with the highest Mountains; above Thirty Thousand Rivers, and Rivulets water her Coasts,

Twelve of which prodigious Number do not yield in all in magnitude to those famous Rivers, the Eber, Duer, and Guadalquivir; and all those Rivers which have their Source or Spring from the Mountains lying Westerly, the number whereof is Twenty Thousand) are very rich in Mines of Gold; on which Mountain lies the Province of rich Mines, whence the exquisite Gold of Twenty Four Caracts weight, takes denomination. The King and Lord of this Kingdom was named Guarionex, who governed within the Compass of his Dominions so many Vassals and Potent Lords, that every one of them was able to bring into the Field Sixteen Thousand Soldiers for the service of Guarionex their Supream Lord and Soverain, when summoned thereunto. Some of which I was acquainted with. This was a most Obedient Prince, endued with great Courage and Morality, naturally of a Pacifick Temper, and most devoted to the service of the Castilian Kings. This King commanded and ordered his Subjects, that every one of those Lords under his Jurisdiction, should present him with a Bell full of Gold; but in succeeding times, being unable to perform it, they were commanded to cut it in two, and fill one part therewith, for the Inhabitants of this Isle were altogether inexperienced, and unskilful in Mine-works, and the digging Gold out of them. This Caiu proferred his Service to the King of Castile, on this Condition, that he would take care, that those Lands should be cultivated and manur'd, wherein, during the reign of Isabella, Queen of Castile, the Spaniards first set footing and fixed their Residence, extending in length even to Santo Domingo, the space of Fifty Miles. For he declar'd (nor was it a Fallacie, but an absolute Truth,) that his Subjects understood not the practical use of digging in Golden Mines. To which promises he had readily and voluntarily condescended, to my own certain knowledge, and so by this means, the King would have received the Annual Revenue of Three Millions of Spanish Crowns, and upward, there being at that very time in that Island Fifty Cities more ample and spacious than Sevil it self in Spain.

But what returns by way of Remuneration and Reward did they make this so Clement and Benign Monarch, can you imagine, no other but this? They put the greatest Indignity upon him imaginable

14

in the person of his Consort who was violated by a Spanish Captain altogether unworthy of the Name of Christian. He might indeed probably expect to meet with a convenient time and opportunity of revenging this Ingominy so unjuriously thrown upon him by preparing Military Forces to attaque him, but he rather chose to abscond in the Province De los Ciquayos (wherein a Puissant Vassal and subject of his Ruled) devested of his Estate and Kingdom, and there live and dye an exile. But the Spaniards receiving certain information, that he had absented himself, connived no longer at his Concealment but raised War against him, who had received them with so great humanity and kindness, and having first laid waste and desolate the whole Region, at last found, and took him Prisoner, who being bound in Fetters was convey'd on board of a ship in order to his transfretation to Castile, as a Captive: but the Vessel perished in the Voyage, wherewith many Spaniards were also lost, as well as a great weight of Gold, among which there was a prodigious Ingot of Gold, resembling a large Loaf of Bread, weighing 3600 Crowns; Thus it pleased God to revenge their enormous impieties.

A Second Kingdom was named Marien, where there is to this day a Haven, upon the utmost Borders of the Plain or open Countrey toward the North, more fertil and large than the kingdom of Portugal; and really deserving constant and frequent Inahbitants: For it abounds with Mountains, and is rich in Mines of Gold and Orichalcum, a kind of Copper Mettal mixt with Gold; The Kings name of this place was Guacanagari, who had many powerful Lords (some whereof were not unknown to me) under his subjection. The first that landed in this Kingdom when he discovered America was an Admiral well stricken in years, who had so hospitable and kind a reception from the aforesaid Gracanagari, as well as all those Spaniards that accompanied him in that Voyage, giving them all imaginable help and assisstance (for the admiral's vessel was sunk on their Coasts) that I heard it from his own mouth, he could not possibly have been entertained with greater Caresses and Civilities from his own parents in his own Native Country. But this King being forced to fly to avoid the Spanish slaughter and Cruelty, deprived of all he was Master of, died in the Mountains; and all the rest of the Potentates and Nobles, his subjects, perished in that servitude and Vassalage; as you shall find in this following Treatise.

The Third Kingdom was distinguished by the Appellation of Maquana, another admirable, healthful and fruitful Region, where at present the most refined sugar of the Island is made. Caonabo then reigned there, who surmounted all the rest in Power, State, and the splendid Ceremonies of His Government. This King beyond all expectation was surpriz'd in his own Palace, by the great subtilty and industry of the Spaniards, and after carried on board in order to his transportation to Castile, but there being at that time six Ships Riding in the Haven, and ready to set Sail such an impetuous storm suddenly arose, that they as well as the Passengers and Ships Crew were all lost, together with King Canabao loaded with Irons; by which judgement the Almighty declared that this was as unjust and impious an Act as any of the former. This Kind had three or four Brothers then Living, Men of strength and Valour, who being highly incensed at the Captivity of their King and Brother, to which he was injuriously reduc'd, having also intelligence of the Devastations and Butcheries committed by the Spaniards in other Regions, and not long after hearing of their Brothers death, took up Arms to revenge themselves of the Enemy, whom the Spaniards met with, and certain party of Horse (which proved very offensive to the Indians) made such havoc and slaughter among them, that the half of this Kingdom was laid waste and depopulated.

Xaraqua is the Fourth Kingdom, and as it were the Centre and Middle of the whole Island, and is not to be equalled for fluency of Speech and politeness of Idiom or Dialect by any Inhabitants of the other Kingdoms, and in Policy and Morality transcends them all. Herein the Lords and Peers abounded, and the very Populace excelled in in stature and habit of Body: Their King was Behechio by name and who had a Sister called Anacaona, and both the Brother as well as Sister had loaded the Spaniards with Benefits and singular acts of Civility, and by delivering them from the evident and apparent danger of Death, did signal services to the Castilian Kings. Behechio dying the supreme power of the Kingdom fell to Anacaona: But it hapned one day, that the Governour of an Island, attended by 60 Horse, and 30 Foot (now the Cavalry was sufficiently able to unpeople not only the Isle, but also the whole Continent) he summoned about 300 Dynasta's, or Noblemen to appear before him, and commanded the most powerful of them, being first crouded into a Thatcht Barn or Hovel, to be exposed to the fury of the merciless Fire, and the rest to be pierced with Lances, and run through with the point of the Sword, by a multitude of Men: And Anacaona her self who (as we said before,) sway'd the Imperial Scepter, to her greater honor was hanged on a Gibbet. And if it fell out that any person instigated by Compassion or Covetousness, did entertain any Indian Boys and mount them on Horses, to prevent their Murder, another was appointed to follow them, who ran them through the back or in the hinder parts, and if they chanced to escape Death, and fall to the ground, they immediately cut off his Legs; and when any of those Indians, that survived these Barbarous Massacres, betook themselves to an Isle eight miles distant, to escape their Butcheries, they were then committed to servitude during Life.

The Fifth Kingdom was Hiquey, over whom Queen Hiquanama, a superannuated Princess, whome the Spaniards Crucified, did preside and Govern. The number of those I saw here burnt, and dismembered, and rackt with various Torments, as well as others, the poor Remnants of such matchless Villanies, who surviving were enslaved, is infinite. But because so much might be said concerning the Assassinations and Depopulating of these people, as cannot without great difficulty be published in Writing (nor do I conceive that one fragile part of 1000 that is here contained can be fully displayed) I will only add one remark more of the prementioned Wars, in lieu of a Corollary or Conclusion, and aver upon my Conscience, that notwithstanding all the above-named Injustice, profligate Enormities and other Crimes which I omit, (tho sufficiently known to me) the Indians did not, nor was it in their power to give any greater occasion for the Commission of them, than

Pious Religioso's Living in a well regulated Monastic Life did afford for any Sacrilegeous Villains to deprive them of their Goods and Life at the same time, or why they who by flight avoided death should be detain'd in perpetual, not to be ransom'd Captivity and Slavery. I adde farther, that I really believe, and am satisfied by certain undeniable conjectures, that at the very juncture of time, when all these outrages were commited in this Isle, the Indians were not so much guilty of one single mortal sin of Commission against the Spaniards, that might deserve from any Man revenge or require satisfaction. And as for those sins, the punishment whereof God hath reserved to himself, as the immoderate desire of Revenge, Hatred, Envy or inward rancor of Spirit, to which they might be transported against such Capital Enemies as the Spaniards were, I judge that very few of them can justly be accused of them; for their impetuosity and vigor I speak experimentally, was inferior to that of Children of ten or twelve years of age: and this I can assure you, that the Indians had ever a just cause of raising War against the Spaniards, and the Spaniards on the contrary never raised a just was against them, but what was more injurious and groundless then any undertaken by the worst of Tyrants. All which I affirm of all their other Transactions and passages in America.

The Warlike Engagements being over, and the Inhabitants all swept away, they divided among themselves the Young Men, Women, and Children reserved promiscuously for that purpose, one obtained thirty, another forty, to this Man one hundred were disposed, to the other two hundred, and the more one was in favor with the domineering Tyrant (which they styled Governor) the more he became Master of, upon this pretence, and with this Proviso, that he should see them instructed in the Catholick Religion, when as they themselves to whom they were committed to be taught, and the care of their Souls instructed them were, for the major part Idiots, Cruel, Avaritious, infected and stained with all sorts of Vices. And this was the great care they had of them, they sent the Males to the Mines to dig and bring away the Gold, which is an intollerable labor; but the Women they made use of to Manure and Till the ground, which is a toil most irksome even to Men of the strongest and most robust constitutions, allowing them no other food but Herbage, and such kind of unsubstantial nutriment, so that the Nursing Womens Milk was exsiccated and so dryed up, that the young Infants lately brought forth, all perished, and females being separated from and debarred cohabitation with Men, there was no Prolification or raising up issue among them. The Men died in Mines, hunger starved and oppressed with labor, and the Women perished in the Fields, harrassed and broken with the like Evils and Calamities: Thus an infinite number of Inhabitants that formerly peopled this Island were exterminated and dwindled away to nothing by such Consumptions. They were compelled to carry burthens of eighty or one hundred pound weight, and that an hundred or two hundred miles compleat: and the Spaniards were born by them on the Shoulders in a pensil Vehicle or Carriage, or kind of Beds made of Net-work by the Indians; for in Truth they made use of them as Beasts to carry the burthens and cumbersom baggage of their journeys, insomuch that it frequently happened, that the Shoulders and Backs of the Indians were deeply marked with their scourges and stripes, just as they used to serve a tired Jade, accustomed to burthens. And as to those slashes with whips, blows with staves, cuffs and boxes, maledictions and curses, with a Thousand of such kind of Torments they suffered during the fatigue of their laborious journeys it would require a long tract of time, and many Reams of Paper to describe them, and when all were done would only create Horror and Consternation in the Reader.

But here is is observable, that the desolation of these Isles and Provinces took beginning since the decease of the most Serene Queen Isabella, about the year 1504, for before that time very few of the Provinces situated in that Island were oppressed or spoiled with unjust Wars, or violated with general devastation as after they were, and most if not all these things were concealed and masked from the Queens knowledge (whom I hope God hath crowned with Eternal Glory) for she was transported with fervent and wonderful zeal, nay, almost Divine desires for the Salvation and preservation of these people, which things so exemplary as these we having seen with our eyes, and felt with our hands, cannot easily be forgotten.

Take this also for a general Rule, that the Spaniards upon what American Coasts soever they arrived, exercised the same Cruelties, Slaughters, Tyrannies and detestable Oppressions on the most innocent Indian Nation, and diverting themselves with delights in new sorts of Torment, did in time improve in Barbarism and Cruelty; wherewith the Omnipotent being incensed suffered them to fail by a more desperate and dangerous lapse into a reprobate state.

Of the Isles of St. John and Jamaica

In the Year 1509, the Spaniards sailed to the Islands of St. John and Jamaica (resembling Gardensa and Bee-hives) with the same purpose and design they proposed to themselves in the Isle of Hispaniola, perpetrating innumerable Robberies and Villanies as before; whereunto they added unheard of Cruelties by Murdering, Burning, Roasting, and Exposing Men to be torn to pieces by Dogs; and Finally by afflicting and harassing them with un-exampled Oppressions and torments in the Mines, they spoiled and unpeopled this Contrey of these Innocents. These two Isles containing six hundred thousand at least, though at this day there are scarce two hundred men to be found in either of them, the remainder perishing without the knowledge of Christian Faith or Sacrament.

Of the Isle of Cuba

In the Year of our Lord 1511. They passed over to Cuba, which contains as much ground in length as there is distance between Valledolid and Rome, well furnished with large and stately Provinces and very populous, against whom they proceeded with no more humanity and Clemency, or indeed to speak truth with greater Savageness and Brutality. Several memorable Transactions worthy observation, passed in this Island. A certain Cacic a potent Peer, named Hathney, who not long before fled Hispaniola to Cuba for

Refuge from Death, or Captivity during Life; and understanding by certain Indians that the Spaniards intended to steer their course thither, made this Oration to all his People Assembled together.

You are not ignorant that there is a rumor spread abroad among us of the Spaniards Arrival, and are sensible by woeful experience how such and such (naming them) and Hayti (so they term Hispaniola in their own language) with their Inhabitants have been treated by them, that they design to visit us with equal intentions of committing such acts as they have hitherto been guilty of. But do you not know the cause and reason of their coming? We are altogether ignorant of it, they replied, but sufficiently satisfied that they are cruelly and wickedly inclined: Then thus, he said, they adore a certain Covetous Deity, whose cravings are not to be satisfied by a few moderate offerings, but they may answer his Adoration and Worship, demand many unreasonable things of us, and use their utmost endeavors to subjugate and afterwards murder us. Then taking up a Cask or Cabinet near at hand, full of Gold and Gems, he proceeded in this manner: This is the Spaniards God, and in honour of him if you think well of it, let us celebrate our Arcytos (which are certain kinds of Dances and caprings used among them); and by this means his Deity being appeas'd, he will impose his Commands on the Spaniards that they shall not for the future molest us; who all unanimously with one consent in a loud tone made this reply. Well said, Well said, and thus they continued skipping and dancing before this Cabinet, without the least intermission, till they were quite tired and grown weary: Then the Noble Hathney re-assuming his discourse, said, if we Worship this Deity, till ye be ravished from us, we shall be destroyed, therefore I judge it convenient, upon mature deliberation, that we cast it into the River, which advice was approved of by all without opposition, and the Cabinet thrown in to the next River.

When the Spaniards first touched this Island, this Cacic, who was thoroughly acquainted with them, did avoid and shun them as much as in him lay, and defended himself by force of Arms, wherever he met with them, but at length being taken he was burnt alive, for flying from so unjust and cruel a Nation, and endeavuoring to secure his Life against them, who only thirsted after the blood of himself and his own People. Now being bound to the post, in order of his Execution a certain Holy Monk of the Franciscan Order, discours'd with him concerning God and the Articles of our Faith, which he never heard of before, and which might be satisfactory and advantagious to him, considering the small time allow'd him by the Executioner, promising him Eternal Glory and Repose, if he truly believ'd them, or other wise Everlasting Torments. After that Hathney had been silently pensive sometime, he askt the Monk whether the Spaniards also were admitted into Heaven, and he answering that the Gates of Heaven were open to all that were Good and Godly, the Cacic replied without further consideration, that he would rather go to Hell then Heaven, for fear he should cohabit in the same Mansion with so Sanguinary and Bloody a Nation. And thus God and the Holy Catholick Faith are Praised and Reverenced by the Practices of the Spaniards in America.

Once it so hapned, that the Citizens of a Famous City, distant Ten Miles from the place where we then resided, came to meet us with a splendid Retinue, to render their Visit more Honourable, bringing with them delicious Viands, and such kind of Dainties, with as great a quantity of Fish as they could possibly procure, and distributing them among us; but behold on a sudden, some wicked Devil possessing the minds of the Spaniards, agitated them with great fury, that I being present, and without the least Pretence or Occasion offered, they cut off in cold Blood above Three Thousand Men, Women and Children promiscuously, such Inhumanities and Barbarisms were committed in my sight, as no Age can parallel.

Some time after I dispatch Messengers to all the Rulers of the Province of Havana, that they would by no means be terrified, or seek their refuge by absence and flight, but to meet us, and that I would engage (for they understood my Authority) that they should not receive the least of Injuries; for the whole Country was extremely afflicted at the Evils and Mischiefs already perpetrated, and this I did with the advice of their Captain. As soon as we approached the Province, Two and Twenty of their Noblemen came forth to meet us, whom the Captain contrary to his Faith given, would have expos'd to the Flames, alledging that it was expedient they should be put to Death, who were, at any time, capacitated to use any Stratagem against us, but with great difficulty and much adoe, I snatcht them out of the fire.

These Islanders of Cuba, being reduc'd to the same Vasselage and Misery as the Inhabitants of Hispaniola, seeing themselves perish and dy without any redress, fled to the Mountains for shelter, but other Desperado's, put a period to their days with a Halter, and the Husband, together with his Wife and Children, hanging himself, put an end to those Calamities.

By the ferocity of one Spanish Tyrant (whom I knew) above Two Hundred Indians hang'd themselves of their own accord; and a multitude of People perished by this kind of Death.

A certain Person here in the same Isle constituted to exercise a kind of Royal Power, hapned to have Three Hundred Indians fall to his share, of which in Three Months, through excessive labour, One Hundred and Sixty were destroy'd, insomuch that in a short space there remained but a tenth part alive, namely Thirty, but when the number was doubled, they all perisht at the same rate, and all that were bestow'd upon him lost their lives, till at length he paid his last Debt to Nature and the Devil.

In Three or Four Months time I being there present, Six Thousand Children and upward were murder'd, because they had lost their Parents
who labour'd in the Mines; nay I was a Witness of many other stupendous
Villanies.

But afterward they consulted how to persecute those that lay hid in the Mountains, who were miserably massacred, and consequently this Isle made desolate, which I saw not long after, and certainly it is a dreadful and depolorable sight to behold it thus unpeopled and laid waste, like a Desert.

Of the Continent

In the Year 1514, a certain unhappy Governour Landed on the firm Land or Continent, a most bloody Tyrant, destitute of all Mercy and Prudence, the Instrument of God's Wrath, with a Resolution to people these parts with Spaniards; and although some Tyrants had touched here before him, and Cruelty hurried them into the other World by several wayes of Slaughter, yet they came no farther than to the Sea Coast, where they comitted podigious Thefts and Robberies, but this Person exceeded all that ever dwelt in other Islands, though execrable and profligate Villains: for he did not only ravage and depopulate the Sea-Coast, but buried the largest Regions and most ample Kingdoms in their own Ruins, sending Thousdands to Hell by his Butcheries. He made Incursions for many Miles continuance, that is to say, in those Countries that are included in the Territories of Darien and the Provinces of Nicaraqua, where are near Five Hundred Miles of the most Fertil Land in the World, and the most opulent for Gold of all the Regions hitherto discover'd. And although Spain has bin sufficiently furnished with the purest Gold, yet it was dig'd out of the Bowels and Mines of the said Countries by the Indians, where (as we have said) they perished.

This Ruler, with his Complices found out new inventions to rack, torment, force and extort Gold from the Indians. One of his Captains in a certain Excursion undertaken by the Command of his Governeur to make Depraedations, destroy'd Forty Thousand Persons and better exposing them to the edge of the Sword, Fire, Dogs and variety of Torments; of all which a Religious Man of the Order of St. Francis, Franciscus de S. Romano, who was then present was an Eye-Witness.

Great and Injurious was the blindness of those praesided over the Indians; as to the Conversion and Salvation of this People: for they denied in Effect what they in their flourishing Discourse pretended to, and declar'd with their Tongue what they contradicted in their Heart; for it came to this pass, that the Indians should be commanded on the penalty of a bloody War, Death, and perpetual Bondage, to embrace the Christian Faith, and submit to the Obedience of the Spanish King; as if the Son of God, who suffered Death for the Redemption of all Mankind, had enacted a Law, when he pronounced these words, Go and teach all Nations that Infidels, living peaceably and quietly in their Hereditary Native Country, should be impos'd upon pain of Confiscation of all their Chattels, Lands, Liberty, Wives, Children, and Death itself, without any precedent instruction to Confess and Acknowledge the true God, and subject themselves to a King, whom they never saw, or heard mention'd before; and whose Messengers behav'd themselves toward them with such Inhumanity and Cruelty as they had done hitherto. Which is certainly a most foppish and absurd way of Proceeding, and merits nothing but Scandal, Derision, nay Hell itself. Now suppose this Notorious and Profligate Governour had bin impower'd to see the Execution of these Edicts perform'd, for of themselves they were repugnant both to Law and Equity; yet he commanded (or they who were to see the Execution thereof, did it of their own Heads without Authority) that when they phansied or proposed to themselves any place, that was well stor'd with Gold, to rob and feloniously steal it away from the Indians living in their Cities and Houses, without the least suspicion of any ill Act. These wicked Spaniards, like Theives came to any place by stealth, half a Mile off of any City, Town or Village, and there in the Night published and proclaim'd the Edict among themselves after this manner:

You Cacics and Indians of this Continent, the Inhabitants of such a Place, which they named; We declare or be it known to you all, that there is but one God, one hope, and one King of Castile, who is Lord of these Countries; appear forth without delay, and take the oath of Allegiance to the Spanish King, as his Vassals.

So about the Fourth Watch of the Night, or Three in the Morning these poor Innocents overwhelm'd with heavy Sleep, ran violently on that place they named, set Fire to their Hovels, which were all thatcht, and so, without Notice, burnt Men, Women and Children; kill'd whom they pleas'd upon the Spot; but those they preserv'd as Captives, were compell'd throughTorments to confess where they had hid the Gold, when they found little or none at their Houses; but they who liv'd being first stigmatized, were made Slaves; yet after the Fire was extinguisht, they came hastily in quest of the Gold. Thus did this Wicked Man, devoted to all the Infernal Furies, behave himself with the Assistance of Profligate Christians, whom he had lifted in his Service from the 14th to the 21. or 22. Year, together with his Domestick Servants and Followers, from whom he received as many Portions, besides what he had from his Slaves in Gold, Pearls, and Jewels, as the Chief Governor would have taken, and all that were constituted to execute any kind of Kingly Office followed in the same Footsteps; every one sending as many of his Servants as he could spare, to share in the spoil. Nay he that came hither as Biship first of all did the same also, And at the vory time (as I conjecture) the Spaniards did depraedate or rob this Kingdom of above Ten Hundred Thousand Crowns of Gold: Yet all these their Thefts and Felonies, we scarce find upon Record that Three Hundred Thousand Castilian Crowns ever came into the Spanish King's Coffers; yet there were above Eight Hundred Thousand Men slain: The other Tyrants who governed this Kingdom afterward to the Three and Thirtieth year, depriv'd all of them of Life that remain'd among the Inhabitants.

Among all those flagitious Acts committed by this Governour while he rul'd this Kindom, or by his Consent and Permission this must by no means be omitted: A certain Casic, bestowing on him a Gift, voluntarily, or (which is more probably) induced thereunto by Fear, about the weight of Nine Thousand Crowns, but the Spaniards not satisfied with so fast a Sum of Money, sieze him, fix him to a Pole; extended his Feet, which being mov'd near the Fire, they demanded a larger Sum; the Casic overcome with Torments, sending home, procur'd Three Thousand more to be brought and presented to them: But the Spaniards, adding new Torments to new Rage and Fury, when they found he would confer no more upon them, which was because he could not, or otherwize because he would not, they expos'd him for so long to that Torture, till by degrees of heat the Marrow gusht out of the Soles of his Feet, and so he dyed; Thus they often murder'd the Lords and Nobles which such Torments to Extort the Gold from them.

One time it hapned that a Century or Party of One Hundred Spaniards making Excursions, came to a Mountain, where many People shunning so horrid and pernicious an Enemy conceal'd themselves, who immediately rushing on them, putting all to the Sword they could meet with, and then secur'd Seventy or Eighty Married Women as well as Virgins Captives; but a great Number of Indians with a fervent desire of recovering their Wives and Daughters appear'd in Arms against the Spaniards, and when they drew near the Enemy, they unwilling to lose the Prey, run the Wives and Maidens through with their Swords. The Indians through Grief and Trouble, smiting their Breasts, brake out into these Exclamations. O perverse Generation of Men! O Cruel Spaniards! What do you Murder las Iras? (In their Language they call Women by the Name of las Iras as if they had said: To slay Women is an Act of bloody minded Men, worse than Brutes and Wild Beasts.

There was the House of a Puissant Potentate scituated about Ten or Fifteen Miles from Panama, whose name was Paris, very Rich in Gold; and the Spaniards gave him a visit, who were entertained with Fraternal Kindness, and Courteously received, and of his own accord, presented the Captain with a Gift of Fifteen Thousand Crowns; who was of opinion, as well as the rest of the Spaniards, that he who bestow'd such a quantity of Money gratis, was the Master of vast Treasure; whereupon they counterfeit a pretended

Departure, but returning about the Fourth Night-Watch, and entring the City privily upon a surprize, which they thought was sufficiently secur'd, consecrated it with many Citizens to the Flames, and robb'd them of Fifty or Sixty Thousand Crowns. The Dynast or Prince escaped with his Life, and gathering together as great a Number of Men as he could possibly at that instant of time, and Three or Four Days being elapsed, pursued the Spaniards, who had depriv'd him also by Violence and Rapine of a Hundred and Thirty or Forty Thousand Crowns, and pouring in upon them, recover'd all his Gold with the destruction of Fifty Spaniards, but the remainder of them having receiv'd many Wounds in that Rencounter betook them to their Heels and sav'd themselves by flight: but in few days after the Spaniards return, and fall upon the said Casic well-arm'd and overthrow him and all his Forces, and they who out-liv'd the Combat, to their great Misfortune, were expos'd to the usual and frequently mention'd Bondage.

Of the Province of Nicaraqua

The said Tyrant An. Dom. 1522. proceeded farther very unfortunately to the Subjugation of Conquest of this Province. In truth no Person can satisfactorily or sufficiently express the Fertility, Temperateness of the Climate, or the Multitude of the Inhabitants of Nicaraqua, which was almost infinite and admirable; for this Region contain'd some Cities that were Four Miles long; and the abundance of Fruits of the Earth (which was the cause of such a Concourse of People) was highly commendable. The People of this place, because the Country was Level and Plain, destitute of Mountains, so very delightful and pleasant, that they could not leave it without great grief, and much dissatisfaction, they were therefore tormented with the greater Vexations and Persecutions, and forced to bear the Spanish Tyranny and Servitude, which as much Patience as they were Masters of: Add farther that they were peaceable and meek spirited. This Tyrant with these Complices of his Cruelty did afflict this Nation (whose advice he made use of in destroying the other Kingdoms) with such and so many great Dammages, Slaughters,

Injustice, Slaver, and Barbarisme, that a Tongue, though of Iron, could not express them all fully. He sent into the Province (which is larger than the County of Ruscinia) Fifty Horse-Men, who put all the People to the Edge of the Sword, sparing neither Age nor Sex upon the most trivial and inconsiderable occasion: As for Example, if they did not come to them with all possible speed, when called; and bring the imposed burthen of Mahid (which signifies Corn in their Dialect) or if they did not bring the Number of Indians required to his own, and the Service or rather Servitude of his Associates. And the Country being all Campaign or Level, no Person was able to withstand the Hellish Fury of their Horses.

He commanded the Spaniards to make Excursions, that is, to rob other Provinces, permitting and granting these Theiving Rogues leave to take away by force as many of these peacable People as they could, who being iron'd (that they might not sink under the Burthen of Sixty or Eighty Pound weight) it frequently hapned, that of Four Thousand Indians, Six only returned home, and so they dyed by the way; but if any of them chanced to faint, being tired with over-weighty Burthens, or through great Hunger and Thirst should be siezed with a Distemper; or too much Debility and Weakness, that they might not spend time in taking off their Fetters, they beheaded them, so the Head fell one way, and the Body another: The Indians when they spied the Spaniards making preparations for such Journeys, knowing very well, that few, or none returned home alive, just upon their setting out with Sighs and Tears, burst out into these or the like Expressions.

Those were Journeys, which we travelled frequently in the service of
Christians, and in some tract of time we return'd to our Habitations,
Wives and Children: But now there being no hope of a return, we are for
ever depriv'd of their Sight and Conversation.
It hapned also, that the same President would dissipate or disperse the Indians de novo at his own pleasure, to the end (as it was

reported) he might violently force the Indians away from such as did infest or molest him; and dispose of them to others; upon which it fell out, that for the space of a Year complete, there was no sowing or planting: And when they wanted Bread, the Spaniards did by force plunder the Indians of the whole stock of Corn that they had laid up for the support of their Families, and by these indirect Courses above Thirty Thousand perished with Hunger. Nay it fortun'd at one time, that a Woman opprest with insufferable Hunger, depriv'd her own Son of his Life to preserve her own.

In this Province also they brought many to an untimely End, loading their Shoulders with heavy planks and pieces of Timer, which they were compell'd to carry to a Haven Forty Miles distant, in order to their building of Ships; sending them likewise unto the Mountains to find out Hony and Wax, where they were devour'd by Tygers; nay they loaded Women impregnated with Carriage and Burthens fit for beasts.

But no greater pest was there that could unpeople this Province, than the License granted the Spaniards by this Governour, to demand Captives from the Casics and Potentates of this Region; for at the Expiration of Four or Five Months, or as often as they obtain'd leave of the Governour to demand them, they deliver'd them up Fifty Servants, and the Spaniards terrified them with Menaces, that if they did not obey them in answering their unreasonable Demands, they should be burnt alive, or baited to Death by Dogs. Now the Indians are but slenderly stor'd with Servants; for it is much if a Casic hath Three or Four in his Retinue, therefore they have recourse to the Subjects; and when they had, in the first place, seized the Orphans, they required earnestly and instantly one Son of the Parent, who had but Two, and Two of him that had but Three, and for the Lord of the place satisfied the desires of the Tyrant, not without the Effusion of Tears and Groans of the People, who (as it seems) were very careful of their Children. And this being frequently repeated in the space between the Year 1523, and 1533, the Kingdom lost all their Inhabitants, for in Six or Seven Years time there were constantly

Five or Six Ships made ready to be fraighted with Indians that were sold in the Regions of Panama and Perusium, where they all dyed; for it is by dayly Experience prov'd and known, that the Indians when Transported out of their Native Country into any other, soon dye; because they are shortned in their allowance of Food, and the Task impos'd on them no ways dimished, they being only bought for Labour. And by this means, there have been taken out of this Province Five Hundred Thousand Inhabitants and upward, who before were Freemen, and made Slaves, and in the Wars made on them, and the horrid Bondage they were reduc'd unto Fifty or Sixty Thousand more have perished, and to this day very many still are destroy'd. Now all these Slaughters have been committed within the space of Fourteen years inclusively, possibly in this Province of Nicaraqua there remains Four or Five Thousand Men who are put to Death by ordinary and personal Opressions, whereas (according to what is said already) it did exceed other Countries of the World in multitude of People.

Of New Spain

New Spain was discovered Anno Dom. 1517. and in the detection there was no first or second Attempt, but all were exposed to slaughter. The year ensuing those Spaniards (who style themselves Christians) came thither to rob, kill and slay, though they pretend they undertook this Voyage to people the Countrey. From this year to the present, viz. 1542. the Injustice, Violence and Tyranny of the Spaniards came to the highest degree of extremety: for they had shook hands with and bid adieu to all fear of God and the King, unmindful of themselves in this sad and deplorable condition, for the Destructions, Cruelties, Butcheries, Devastations, the Domolishing of Cities, Depradations, &c. which they perpetrated in so many and such ample Kingdoms, are such and so great, and strike the minds of Men with so great horror, that all we have related before are inconsiderable comparatively to those which have been acted from the year 1518 to 1542, and to this very month of September that we now live to see the most heavy, grievous and detestable things are committed, that the Rule we laid down before as a Maxim might be induputably verified, to wit, that from the beginning they ran headlong from bad to worse, and were overcome in their Diabolical acts and wickedness only by themselves.

Thus from the first entrance of the Spaniards into New Spain, which hapned on the 18th day of April in the said month of the year 1518, to 1530, the space of ten whole years, there was no end or period put to the Destruction and Slaughters committed by the merciless hands of the Sanguinary and Blood-thirsty Spaniard in the Continent, or space of 450 Miles round about Mexico, and the adjacent or neighboring parts, which might contain four or five spatious Kingdoms, that neither for magnitude or fertility would give Spain her self the pre-eminence. This intire Region was more populous then Toledo, Sevil, Valedolid, Saragoza, and Faventia; and there is not at this day in all of them so many people, nor when they flourisht in their greatest height and splendor was there such a number, as inhabited that Region, which embraceth in its Circumference, four hundred and eighty Miles. Within these twelve years the Spaniards have destroyed in the Said Countinent, by Spears, Fire and Sword, computing Men, Women, Youth, and Children above Four Millions of people in these their Acquests or Conquests (for under that word they mask their Cruel Actions) or rather those of the Turk himself, which are reported of them, tending to the ruin of the Catholick Cause, together with their Invasions and Unjust Wars, contrarty to and condemned by Divine as well as Human Laws; nor are they reckoned in this number who perished by their more then Egyptian Bondage and usual Oppressions.

There is no Tongue, Art, or Human knowledge can recite the horrid Impieties, which these Capital Enemies to Government and all Mankind have been guilty of at several times and in several Nations; nor can the circumstantial Aggravations of some of their wicked Acts be unfolded or display'd by any manner of Industry, time or writing, but yet I will say somewhat of every individual particular thing, which this protestation and Oath, that I conceive I am not able to comprehend one of a Thousand.

Of New Spain in Particular

Among other Slaughters this also they perpetrated in the most spacious City of Cholula, which consisted of Thirty Thousand Families; all the Chief Rulers of that Region and Neighboring places, but first the Priests with their High Priest going to meet the Spaniards in Pomp and State, and to the end they might give them a more reverential and honourable reception appointed them to be in the middle of the Solemnity, that so being entertained in the Appartments of the most powerful and principal Noblemen, they might be lodged in the City. The Spaniards presently consult about their slaughter or castigation (as they term it) that they might fill every corner of this Region by their Cruelties and wicked Deeds with terror and consternation; for in all the Countries that they came they took this course, that immediately at their first arrival they committed some notorious butcheries, which made those Innocent Sheep tremble for fear. To this purpose therefore they sent to the Governours and Nobles of the Cities, and all Places subject unto them, together with their supream Lord, that they should appear before them, and no soner did they attend in expectation of some Capitulation or discourse with the Spanish Commander, but they were presently seized upon and detained prisoners before any one could advertise or give them notice of their Captivity. They demanded of them six thousand Indians to drudge for them in the carriage of their bag and baggage; and as soon as they came the Spaniards clapt them into the Yards belonging to their Houses and there inclosed them all. It was a thing worthy of pity and compassion to behold this wretches people in what a condition they were when they prepared themselves to receive the burthens laid on them by the Spaniards. They came to them naked, their Privities only vail'd, their Shoulders loaden with food; only covered with a Net, they laid themselves quietly on the ground, and shrinking in their Bodies like poor Wretches, exposed themselves to their Swords: Thus being all gathered together in ther Yards, some of the Spaniards Armed held the doors to drive them away if attempting to approach, and others with Lances and Swords Butcher these Innocents so that not one of them escaped, but two or three days after some of them, who hid themselves among the dead bodies, being all over besprinkled with blood and gore, presented themselves to the Spaniards, imporing their mercy and the prolongation of their Lives with tears in their Eyes and all imaginable submission, yet they, not in the least moved with pity or compassion, tore them in pieces: but all the Chief Governours who were above one hundred in number, were kept bound, whom the Captain commanded to be affixed to posts and burnt; yet the King of the whole Countrey escaped, and betook himself with a Train of thirty or forty Gentlemen, to a Temple (called in their Tongue Quu) which he made use of as a Castle or Place of Defence, and there defended himself a great part of the day, but the Spaniards who suffer none to escape out of their clutches, especially Souldiers, setting fire to the Temple, burnt all those that were there inclosed, who brake out into these dying words and exclamations. O profligate Men, what injury have we done you to occasion our death! Go, go to Mexico, where our supream Lord Montencuma will revenge our cause upon your persons. And 'tis reported, while the Spaniards were engated in this Tragedy destroying six or seven thousand Men, that their Commander with great rejoycing sang this following Ayre;

Mira Nero de Tarpeia, Roma como se ardia, Gritos de Ninos y Vieyot, y el de nadase dolia.

From the Tarpeian still Nero espies Rome all in Flames with unrelenting Eyes, And hears of young and old the dreadful Cries.

They also committed a very great Butchery in the City Tepeara, which was larger and better stored with Houses than the former; and here they Massacred an incredible number with the point of the Sword.

Setting sail from Cholula, they steer'd their course to Mexico, whose King sent his Nobles and Peers with abundance of Presents to meet them by the way, testifying by divers sorts of Recreations how grateful their arrival was and acceptable to him: but when they came to a steep Hill, his brother went forward to meet them accompanied with many Noblemen who brought them many gifts in Gold, Silver, and Robes Emboidered with Gold and at their entrance into the City, the King himself carried in a golden Litter, together (with the whole Court) attended them to the Palace prepared for their reception; and that very day as I was informed by some persons then and there present by a grand piece of Treachery, they took the very great King Montencuma, never so much as dreaming of any such surprize, and put him into the custody of eighty Soldiers, and afterward loaded this Legs with irons; but all these things being passed over with a light pencil of which much might be said, one thing I will discover acted by them, that may merit your obervation. When the Captain arrived at the Haven, to fight with a Spanish Officer, who made War against him, and left another with an hundred Soldiers, more or less as a Guard to King Montencuma, it came into their heads, that to act somewhat worth remembrance, that the dread of their Cruelty might be more and more apprehended, and greatly increased.

In the interim all the Nobility and Commonality of the City thought of nothing else, but how to exhilarate the Spirit of their Captive King, and solace him during his Confinement with varity of diversions and Recreations; and among the rest this was one, viz., Revellings and Dances which they celebrated in all Streets and Highways, by night and they in their Idiom term Mirotes, as the Islanders do Arcytos; to these Masques and nocturnal Jigs they usually go with all their Riches, Costly Vestments and Robes, together with any thing that is pretious and glorious, being wholly addicted to this humor, nor is there any greater token among them then this of their extraordinary exultation and rejoycing. The Nobles in like manner, and Princes of the Blood Royal every one according to his degree exercise these Masques and Dances, in some place adjoyning to the House where their King and Lord is detained Prisoner. Now there were not far from the Palace about 2000 Young Noblemen who were the issue of the greatest Potentates of the Kingom, and indeed the flower of the whole Nobility of King Motencuma, and a Spanish Captain went to visit them with some Soldiers, and sent others to the rest of the places in the City where these Revellings were kept, under pretence only of being spectators of the solemnity. Now the Captain had commanded, that, at a certain hour appointed they should fall upon these Revellers, and he himself approaching the Indians very busie at their Dancing, said, San Jago (that is St. James it seems that was the Word) Let us rush in upon them, which was no sooner heard, but they all began with their naked Swords in hand to pierce their tender and naked Bodies, and spill their generous and Noble blood, till not one of them was left alive on the place, and the rest following his example in other parts, (to their inexpressible stupefaction and grief) seized on all these Provinces. Nor will the Inhabitants till the General conflagration ever discontinue the Celebration of these Festivals, and the Lamentation and Singing with certain kind of Rhythmes in their Arcytos, the doleful ditty of the Calamity and Ruin of this Seminary of the antient Nobility of the whole Kingdom, which was their frequent Pride and Glory.

The Indians seeing this not to be exampled cruelty and iniquity executed against such a number of guiltless persons, and also bearing with incredible patience the unjust Imprisonment of their King, from whom they had an absolute Command not to take up Arms against the Spaniard, the whole City was suddenly up in Arms fell on the Spaniards and wounded many of them, the rest hardly escaping; but they presenting the point of a Sword to the Kings Breast, threatned him with death unless he out of the Window commanded them to desist; but the Indians for the present disobeying the Kings Mandate, proceeded to the Election of a Generalissimo, or Commander in Chief over all their Forces; and because that the Captain, who went to the Port returned Victor, and brought away a far greater number of Spaniards then he took along with him, there was a Cessation of Arms for three or four days, till he re-entred the City, and then the Indians having gatherered together and made up a great Army, fought so long and so strenuously, that the Spaniards despairing of their safety, called a Council of War and therein resolv'd to retreat in the dead time of night and so draw off their Forces from the City: which coming to the knowledge of the Indians they destroyed a great number Retreating on the Bridges made over their Lakes in this just and Holy War, for the causes above-mentioned, deserving the approbation of every upright Judge. But afterward the Spaniards having recruited and got together in a Body, they resolved to take the City and carried it at last, wherein most detestable Butcheries were acted, a vast number of the people slain, and their Rulers perished in the Flames.

All these horrid Muders being commited in Mexico and other Cities ten, fifteen and twenty miles distant. This same Tyranny and Plague in the abstract proceeded to infest and lay desolate Panuco; a Region abounding with Inhabitants even to admiration, nor were the slaughters therein perpetrated less stupendous and wonderful. In the same manner they utterly laid wasate the Provinces of Futepeca, Ipilcingonium and Columa, every one of them being as large as the Kingdoms of Leon, and Castile. It would be very difficult or rather impossible to relate the Cruelties and Destruction there made and committed, and prove very nauseous and offensive to the Reader.

'Tis observable, that they entred upon these Dominions and laid waste the Indian Territories, so populous, that it would have rejoyced the hearts of all true Christians to see their number upon no other title or pretense, but only to enslave them; for at their first arrival they compel'd them to swear the Oath of Obedience and Fealty to the King of Spain, and if they did not condescend to it, they menace them with death and Vassalage, and they who did not forthwith appear to satisfie the unequitable Mandates, and submit to the will and pleasure of such unjust and Cruel Men were declared Rebels, and accu's of that Crime before our Lord the King; and blindess or ignorance of those who were set over the Indians as Rulers did so darken their understanding that they did not apprehend that known and incontrovertible Maxim in Law, That no

Man can be called a Rebel, who is not first proved to be a subject. I omit the injuries and prejudice they do to the King himself, when they spoil and ravage his Kingdoms, and as much as in them lies, diminish and impair all his Right and Title to the Indians, nay in plain English invalidate and make it null and void. And these are the worthy Services which the Spaniards do for our Kings in those Countries, by the injust and colourable pretences aforesaid.

This Tyrant upon the same pretext sent two other Captains, who exceeded him in impiety and cruelty, if possible to the most flourishing and Feril (in Fruits and Men) Kingdoms of Guatemala, Situate toward the South, who had also received Orders to go to the Kingdoms of Naco, Hondera, and Guaymura, verging upon the North, and are Borderers on Mexico three hundred miles together. The one was sent by Land and the other by Sea, and both well furnished with Horse and Foot.

This I declare for a Truth, that the outrages committed by these two, particularly by him that went to Guatimala (for the other not long after his departure died a violent Death) would afford matter sufficient for an entire Volume, and when completed he so crouded with slaughters, injuries, butcheries and inhuman Desolations, so horrid and detestable as would Ague-shake the present as well as future ages with terror.

He that put out to Sea vexed all the Maritime Coasts with his cruel Incursions; now some inhabitants of the Kingdom of Jucatan which is seated in the way to the Kingdoms of Naco and Naymura, to which places he steered his course, came to meet him with burthens of Presents and Gifts: and as soon as he approacht them, sent his Captains with a party of Soldiers to depopulate their Land, who committed great spoils and made cruel slaughters among them; and in particular a Seditious and Rebellious Officer who with three hundres Soldiers entred a Neighboring Country to Guatimala, and there firing the Cities and Murdering all the Inhabitants, violently deprived them of all their goods, which he did designedly, for the space of an hundred and twenty miles; to the end that if his Companions should follow them, they might find the Country laid wast, and so be destroyed by the Indians in revenge for the dammage they had received by him and his Forces which hapned accordingly: for the Chief Commander whose order the abovesaid Captain had disobey'd and so became a Rebel to him, was there slain. But many other bloody Tyrants succeeded him, who from the year 1524 to 1535. did unpeople and make a Desert of the Provinces of Naco and Hondura (as well as other places) which were lookt upon as the Paradise of delights, and better peopled then other Regions; insomuch that within the Term of these eleven years there fell in those Countries above two Millions of Men, and now there are hardly remaining Two Thousand, who dayly dye by the severity of their Slavery.

But to return to that great Tyrant, who outdid the former in cruelty (as hinted above) and is equal to those that Tyrannize there at present, who travelled to Guatimala; he from the Provinces adjoyning to Mexico, which according to his prosecuted journey (as he himself Writes and testifies with his own hand in Letters to the Prince of Tyrants) are distant from Guatimala four hundred miles, did make it to his urgent and dayly business to procure Ruin and Destruction by slaughter, Fire and Depopulations, compelling all to submit to the Spanish King, whom they lookt upon to be more unjust and cruel then his inhumane and bloodthirsty Ministers.

Of the Kingdom and Province of Guatimala

This Tyrant at his first entrance here acted and commanded prodigious Slaughters to be perpetrated: Notwithstanding which, the Chief Lord in his Chair or Sedan attended by many Nobles of the City of Ultlatana, the Emporium of the whole Kingdom, together with Trumpets, Drums and great Exultation, went out to meet him, and brought with them all sorts of Food in great abundance, with such things as he stood in most need of. That Night the Spaniards spent without the City, for they did not judge themselves secure in such a well-fortified place. The next day he commanded the said Lord with many of his Peers to come before him, from whom they imperiously challenged a certain quantity of Gold; to whom the Indians return'd this modest Answer, that they could not satisfie his Demands, and indeed this Region yeilded no Golden Mines; but they all, by his command, without any other Crime laid to their Charge, or any Legal Form of Proceeding were burnt alive. The rest of the Nobles belonging to other Provinces, when they found their Chief Lords, who had the Supreme Power were expos'd to the Merciless Element of Fire kindled by a more merciless Enemy; for this Reason only, becauase they bestow'd not what they could not upon them, viz. Gold, they fled to the Mountains, (their usual Refuge) for shelter, commanding their Subjects to obey the Spaniards, as Lords, but withal strictly and expressly prohibiting and forbidding them, to inform the Spaniards of their Flight, or the Places of their Concealment. And behold a great many of the Indians addrest themselves to them, earnestly requesting, they would admit them as Subjects, being very willing and ready to serve them: The Captain replyed that he would not entertain them in such a Capacity, but instead of so doing would put every individual Person to Death, if they would not discover the Receptacles of the Fugitive Governours. The Indians made answer that they were wholly ignorant of the matter, yet that they themselves, their Wives and Children should serve them; that they were at home, they might come to them and put them to Death, or deal with them as they pleas'd. But the Spaniards, O wonderful! went to the Towns and Villages, and destroy'd with their Lances these poor Men, their Wives and Children, intent upon their Labour, and as they thought themselves, secure and free from danger. Another large Village they made desolate in the space of two hours, sparing neither Age, nor Sex, putting all to the Sword, without Mercy.

The Indians perceiving that this Barbarous and Hard-hearted People would not be pacified with Humility, large Gifts, or unexampled Patience, but that they were butcher'd without any Cause, upon serious Consultation took up a Resolution of getting together in a

Body, and fighting for their Lives and Liberty; for they conceiv'd it was far better, (since Death to them was a necessary Evil) with Sword in Hand to be kill'd by taking Revenge of the Enemy, then be destroy'd by them without satisfaction. But when they grew sensible of their wants of Arms, Nakedness and Debility, and that they were altogether incapable of the management of Horses, so as to prevail against such a furious Adversary, recollecting themselves, they contriv'd this Strategm, to dig Ditches and Holes in the High-way into which the Horses might fall in their passage, and fixing therein purposely sharp and burnt Posts, and covering them with loose Earth, so that they could not be discern'd by their Riders, they might be transfixed or gored by them. The Horses fell twice or thrice into those holes, but afterward the Spaniards took this Course to prevent them for the future; and made this a Law, that as many of the Indians of what Age or Sex soever as were taken, should be cast into these Ditches that they had made. Nay they threw into them Women with Child, and as many Aged Men as they laid hold of, till they were all fill'd up with Carkasses. It was a sight deserving Commiseration, to behold Women and Children gauncht or run through with these Posts, some were taken off by Spears and Swords, and the remainder expos'd to hungry Dogs, kept short of food for that purpose, to be devour'd by them and torn in pieces. They burnt a Potent Nobleman in a very great Fire, saying, That he was the more Honour'd by this kind of Death. All which Butcheries continued Seven Years, from 1524, to 1531. I leave the Reader to judge how many might be Massacred during that time.

Among the Innumerable Flagitious Acts done by this Tyrant and his Co-partners (for they were as Barbarous as their Principal) in this Kingdom, this also occurs worthy of an Afterism in the Margin. In the Province of Cuztatan in which S. Saviour's City is seated, which Country with the Neighbouing Sea-Coasts extends in Length Forty or Fifty Miles, as also in the very City of Cuzcatan, the Metropolis of the whole Province, he was entertain'd with great Applause: For about Twenty or Thirty Thousand Indians brought with them Hens and other necessary Provisions, expecting this coming. He, accepting their Gifts, commended every single Spaniard to make choice of as many of these People, as he had a mind to, that during their stay there, they might use them as Servants, and forced to undergo the most servile Offices they should impose on them. Every one cull'd out a Hundred, or Fifty, according as he thought convenient for his peculiar service, and these wretched Indians did serve the Spaniards with their utmost strength and endeavour; so that there could be nothing wanting in them but Adoration. In the mean time this Captain requir'd a great Sum of Gold from their Lords (for that was the Load-stone attracted them thither) who answered, they were content to deliver him up all the Gold they had in possession; and in order thereunto, the Indians gathered together a great Number of Spears gilded with Orichalcum, (which had the appearance of Gold, and in truth some Gold in them intermixt) and they were presented to him. The Captain ordered them to be toucht, and when he found them to be Orichalcum or mixt Metal, he spake to the Spaniards as followeth. Let that Nation that is without Gold be accursed to the Pit of Hell. Let every Man detain those Servants he Elected, let them be clapt in Irons, and stigmatiz'd with the Brand of Slavery, which was accordingly done, for they were all burnt, who did no excape with the King's Mark. I my self saw the Impression made on the Son of the Chiefest Person in the City. Those that escap'd, with other Indians, engaged the Spaniards by Force of Arms, but with such ill success, that abundance of them lost their Lives in the Attempt. After this they return'd to Gautimala, where they built a City, which God in his Judgement with Three Deluges, the First of Water, the Second of Earth, the Third of Stones, as big as half a score Oxen, all concurring at one and the same time, laid Level with its own Ashes. Now all being slain who were capable of bearing Arms against them, the rest were enslav'd, paying so much per Head for Men and Women as a Ransom; for they use no other servitude here, and then they were sent into Pecusium to be sold, by which means together with their slaughters committed upon the Inhabitants, they destroy'd and made a Desert of this Kingdom, which in Breadth as well as Length contains One Hundred Miles; and with his Associates and Brethren in Iniquity, Four Millions at least in Fifteen or Sixteen Years, that is, from 1524, to 1540 were murdered, and dayly continues destroying the small residue of that People with his Cruelties and Brutishness.

It was the usual Custom of this Tyrant, when he made War with any City or Province, to take along with himas many of those Indians he had subjugated as he could, that they might fight with their Country-men; and when he had in his Army Twenty, or sometimes Thirty Thousand of them, and could not afford them sustenance, he permitted them to feed on the Flesh of other Indians taken Prisoners in War; and so kept a Shambles of Man's Flesh in his Army, suffered Children to be kill'd and roasted before his Face. They butcher'd the Men for their Feet and Hands only; for these Members were accounted by them Dainties, most delicious Food.

He as the Death of many by the intolerable Labour of Carrying Ships by Land, causing them to Transport those Vessels with Anchors of a vast weight from the Septentrional to the Mediterranean Sea, which are One Hundred and Thirty Miles distant; as also abundance of great Guns of the largest fort, which they carried on their bare, naked shoulders, so that opprest with many great and ponderous Burthens, (I say no more than what I saw) they dyed by the way: He separated and divided Families, forcing Married Men from their Wives, and Maids from their Parents, which he bestow'd upon his Marriners and Soldiers, to gratifie their burning Lust. All his Ships he freighted with Indians, where Hunger and Thirst discharg'd them of their Servitude and his Cruelty by a welcome Death. He had two Companies of Soldiers who hackt and tore them in pieces, like Thunder from Heaven speedily. O how many Parents has he robb'd of their Children, how many Wives of their Husbands, and Children of their Parents? How many Adulteries, Rapes, and what Libidinous Acts hath he been guilty of? How many hath he enslav'd and opprest with insufferable Anguish and unspeakable Calamities? How many Tears, Sighs and Groans hath he occasion'd? To how many has he bin the Author of Desolation, during their Peregrination in this, and of Damnation in the World to come, not only to Indians, whose Number is numberless, but even to Spaniards themselves, by whose help and assistance he committed such detestable Butcheries and flagitious Crimes? I supplicate Almighty God, that he would please to have Mercy on his Soul, and require no other satisfaction than the violent Death, which turn'd him out of this World.

A farther Discourse of New Spain: And some Account of Panuco and Xalisco

After the perpetration of all the Cruelties rehearsed in New Spain and other places, there came another Rabid and Cruel Tyrant to Panuco, who acted the part of a bloody Tragedian as well as the rest, and sent away many Ships loaden with these Barbarians to be sold for Slaves, made this Province almost a Wilderness, and which was deplorable, Eight Hundred Indians, that had Rational Souls were given in Exchange for a Burthen-bearing-Beast, a Mule, or Camel. Well, He was made Governour of the City of Mexico, and all New Spain, and with him many other Tyrants had the Office of Auditors confer'd upon them: Now they had already made such a progress toward the Desolation of this Region, that if the Franciscans had not vigorously opposed them, and that by (the King's Council, the best and greatest Encourager of Vertue) it had not speedily bin prevented, that which hapned to Hispaniola in Two Years, had bin the Fate of Hispania nova, namely to be unpeopled, deferred, and intomb'd in its own Rules. A Companion of this Governour employed Eight Thousand Indians in Erecting a wall to inclose his Garden, but they all dyed, having no Supplies, nor Wages from him, to support themselves, at whose Death he was not in the least concern'd.

After the first Captain before spoken of had absolutely profliaged and ruin'd the Panuconians, Fifteen Thousand whereof perished by carrying their Bag and Baggage: At length he arriv'd at the Province of Machuacan, which is Forty Miles Journey from Mexico, and as Fertile and Populous: The King to honour him in the Rencounter, with a Multiple of People, marcheth toward him, from whom he had received One Thousand Services and Civilities very considerable, who gratefully requited him with Captivity, because Fame had nois'd it abroad, that he was a most Opulent Prince in Gold and Silver; and to the end he might export from, and purge him of his Gold, he was cruciated with Torments after this manner; his Body was extended, Hands bound to a Post, and his Feet put into a pair of Stocks, they all the while applying burning Coals to his Feet at a tormenting distance, where a Boy attended, who by little and little sprinkled them with Oyl, that his Flesh might roast the better: Before him there stood a Wicked Fellow, presenting a Bow to his Breast charged with a Mortal Arrow, (if let fly) behind him, another with Dogs held in with Chains, which he threatned to let loose at him, which if done, he had bin torn to pieces in a moment; and with these kind of Torments they racked him to extort a Confession, where his Treasures lay; till a Franciscan Monk came and deliver'd him from his Torments, but not from Death, for he departed this miserable Life not long after: And this was the severe Fate of many Cacics and Indian Lords, who dyed with the same Torments which they were expos'd to by the Spaniards, in order to the engrossing of their Gold and Sliver to themselves.

At this very time, A certain Visiter of Purses rather than Souls hapned to be here present, who (finding some Indian Idols which were hid; for they were no better instructed in the Knowledge of the true God by reason of the Wicked Documents and Dealings of the Spaniards) detain'd Grandees as Slaves, till they had deliver'd him all their Idols, for he phancied they were made of Gold or Silver, but his Expectation being frustrated, he chastised them with no less Cruelty than Injustice; and that he might not depart bubbled out of all his hopes, constrain'd them to redeem their Idols with Money, that so they might, according to their Custom, Adore them. These are the Fruits of the Spanish Artifices and Juggling Tricks among the Indians, and thus they promoted the honour and worship of God.

This Tyrant from Mechuacam arrives at Xalisco, a Country abounding with People very fruitful, and the Glory of the Indians in this respect, that it had some Towns Seven Miles long; and among other Barbarisms equal to what you have read, which they acted here, this is not to be forgotten, that Women big with Child, were burthen'd with the Luggage of Wicked Christians, and being unable to go out their usual time, through extremity of Toil and Hunger, were necessitated to bring them forth in the High-wayes, which was the Death of many Infants.

At a certain time a profligate Christian attempted to devirginate a Maid, but the Mother being present, resisted him, and endeavouring to free her from his intended Rape, whereat the Spaniard enrag'd, cut off her Hand with a short Sword, and stab'd the Virgin in several places, till she Expir'd, because she obstinately opposed and disappointed his inordinate Appetite.

In this Kingdom of Xalisco (according to report) they burnt Eight Hundred Towns to Ashes, and for this Reason the Indians growing desperate, beholding the dayly destruction of the Remainders of their matchless Cruelty, made an Insurrection against the Spaniards, slew several of them justly and deservedly, and afterward fled to the insensible Rocks and Mountains (yet more tender and kind than the stony-hearted Enemy) for Sanctuary; where they were miserably Massacred by those Tyrants who succeeded, and there are now few, or none of the Inhabitants to be found. Thus the Spaniards being blinded with the Lustre of their Gold, deserted by God, and given over to a Reprobate Sense, not undrestanding (or at least not willing to do so) that the Cause of the Indians is most Just, as well by the Law of Nature, as the Divine and Humane, they by Force of Arms, destroying them, hacking them in pieces, and turning them out of their own Confines and Dominions, nor considering how unjust those Violences and Tyrannies are, wherewith they have afflicted these poor Creatures, they still contrive to raise new Wars against them: Nay they conceive, and by Word and Writing testifie, that those Victories they have obtain'd against those Innocents to their ruine, are granted them by God himself, as if their unjust Wars were promoted and managed by a just Right and Title to what they pretend; and with boasting Joy return Thanks to God for their Tyranny, in imitation of those Tyrants and Robbers, of whom the

Prophet Zechariah part of the Forth and Fifth Verses. Feed the Sheep of the slaughter, whose Possessors slay them, and hold themselves not guilty, and they that sell them say, Blessed by the Lord, for ye are rich.

Of the Kingdom of Jucatan

An Impious Wretch by his Fabulous Stories and Relations to the King of Spain was made praefect of the Kingdom of Jucatan, in the Year of our Lord 1526; And the other Tyrants to this very day have taken the same indirect Measures to obtain Offices, and screw or wheedle themselves into publick Charges or Employments, for this praetext, and Authority, they had the greater opportunity to commit Theft and Rapine. This Kingdom was very well peopled, and both for Temperature of Air, and the Plenty of Food and Fruits, in which respect it is more Fertile than Mexico, but chiefly for Hony and Wax, it exceeds all the Indian Countries that hath hitherto bin discover'd. It is Three Hundred Miles in Compass. The Inhabitants of this place do much excel all other Indians, either in Politie or Prudence, or in leading a Regular Life and Morality, truly deserving to be instructed in the Knowledge of the true God. Here the Spaniards might have Erected many fair Cities, and liv'd as it were in a Garden of Delights, if they had not, through Covetousness, Stupidity, and the weight of Enormous Crimes rendred themselves unworthy of so great a Benefit. This Tyrant, with Three Hundred Men began to make War with these Innocent People, living peaceably at home, and doing injury to none, which was the ruine of a great Number of them: Now because this Region affords no Gold; and if it did the Inhabitants would soon have wrought away their lives by hard working in the Mines, that so he might accumulate Gold by their bodies and Souls, for which Christ was Crucified: For the generality he made slaves of those whose lives he spared, and sent away such Ships as were driven thither by the Wind of report, loaden with them, exchanging them for Wine, Oyl, Vinegar, Salt Pork, Garments, Pack Horses and other Commodities, which he thought most necessary and fit for his use. He proposed to them the choice of Fifty Virgins, and she that was the fairest or best complexioned he bartered for a small Cask of Wine, Oyl, Vinegar or some inconsiderable quantity of salt Pork, the same exchange he proferred of Two or Three Hundred well-disposed Young Boys, and one of them who had the Mind or presence of a Princes Son, was given up to them for a Cheese, and One Hundred more for a Horse. Thus he continued his flagitious courses from 1526 to 1533, inclusively, till there was news brought of the Wealth and Opulence of the Region of Perusia, whither the Spaniards marcht, and so for some time there was a Cessation of this Tyranny; but in a few days after they returned and acted enormous Crimes, robbed, and imprisoned them and committed higher offences against the God of Heaven; nor have they ye done, so that now these Three Hundred Miles of Land so populous (as I said before) lies now uncultivated and almost deserted.

No Solifidian can believe the particular Narrations of their Barbarism, and Cruelty in those Countreys. I will only relate two or three Stories which are fresh in my memory. The Spaniards used to trace the steps of the Indians, both Men and Women with curst Currs, furious Dogs; an Indian Woman that was sick hapned to be in the way in sight, who perceiving that she was not able to avoid being torn in pieces by the Dogs, takes a Cord that she had and hangs her self upon a Beam, tying her Child (which she unforunately had with her) to her foot; and no sooner had she done, yet the Dogs were at her, tearing the Child, but a Priest coming that way Baptiz'd it before quite dead.

When the Spaniards left this Kingdom, one of them invited the Son of some Indian Governour of a City or Province, to go along with him, who told him he would not leave or desert his Native Countrey, whereupon he threatned to cut off his ears, if he refus'd to follow him: But the Youth persisting resolutely, that he would continue in the place of his Nativity, he drawing his Sword cut off each Ear, notwithstanding which he persever'd in his first opinion, and then as if he had only pincht him, smilingly cut off his Nose and Lips.

This Rogue did lasciviously boast before a Priest, and as if he had merited the greatest applause, commended himself to the very Heavens, saying, "He had made it his chief Trade or Business to impregnate Indian Women, that when they were sold afterward, he might gain the more Money by them."

In this Kingdom or (I'm certain) in some Province of New Spain, A Spaniard Hunting and intent on his game, phancyed that his Beagles wanted food; and to supply their hunger snatcht a young little Babe from the Mothers breast, cutting off his Arms and Legs, cast a part of them to every Dog, which they having devour'd, he threw the remainder of the Body to them. Thus it is plainly manifest how they value these poor Creatures, created after the image of God, to cast them to their Canibal Curs. But that which follows is (if possible) a sin of a deeper dye.

I pretermit their unparallel'd Impieties, &c. and only close all with this one Story that follows. Those haughty obdurate and execrable Tyrants, who departed from this Countrey to Fish for Riches in Perusia, and four Monks of the Order of St. Francis, with Father James who Travelled thither also to keep the Countrey in Peace, and attract or mildly perswade by their Preaching the remnant of Inhabitants, that had outlived a septennial Tyranny, to embrace the knowledge of Christ. I conceive these are the persons who in the year 1534, Travelling by Mexico were sollicited by several Messengers from the Indians, to come into their Countrey, and inform them in the knowledge of one God, the true God, and Lord of the whole World: to this end they appointed Assemblies and Councils to examine and understand what Men they were, who called themselves Fathers and Friers, what they intended and what difference there was between them and the Spaniards, by whom they had been so molested and tormented: but they received them at length upon this condition that they should be admitted alone, without any Spaniards, which the Fathers promised; for they had permission, nay an express Mandate from the President of New Spain to make that promise, and that the Spaniards should not do them the least detriment or injury. Then they began, to Preach the Gospel of Christ, and to explicate and declare the pious intention of the King of Castile, of all which they had notice by the Spaniards for seven years together, that they had no King nor no other but him, who oppressed them with so much Tyranny. The Priests continued there but forty days, but behold they bring forth all their Idols to be committed to the flames; and then their Children which they tendred as the apple of the Eye, that they might be instructed. They also erected Temples and Houses for them and they were desired to come to other Provinces and Preach the Gospel, and introduce them into the knowledge of God, and the Great (as they stiled him) King of Castile: And the Priests perswasions wrought so effectually on them, that they condescended to that which was never done in India before (for whatsoever those Tyrants who wasted and consumed these large Kingdoms and Provinces, did misrepresent and falsifie, was only done to bring an odium and disgrace upon the Indians). For Twelve or Fifteen Princes of spatious and well-peopled Regions assembled, every one distinct and separate from the rest, with his own subjects, and by their unanimous consent upon Council and Advice, of their own accord sumitted themselves to the Government of the Castilian Kings and accepted of them as their Prince and Protector, obliging themselves to obey and serve them as subjects to their Lawful Liege Lord.

In Witness whereof I have in my custody, a certain Instrument Signed and Attested by the aforesaid Religioso's.

Thus to the great joy and hope of these Priests reducing them to the knowledge of Christ they were received by the Inhabitants of this Kingdom, that surviv'd the heat and rage of the Spanish Cruelties: but behold eighteen Horse and Twelve Footmen by another way crept in among them, bringing with them many Idols, which were of great weight, and taken out of other Regions by Force. The Commander in chief of these Spaniards summoned one of the Dynasts or Rulers of that Province which they entred into, to appear before him, and command him to take these Idols with him, distribute them through his Countrey and exchange every single Idol for an Indian Man or Woman, otherwise he would make War against him. The abovesaid Lord compelled to it by fear did so accordingly with a command, that his Subjects should adore Worship and Honour them, and in compensation send Indians Male and Female into servitude. The terrified People delivered up their Children, and by this means there was an end made of this Sacrilegious Merchandize, and thus the Casic satisfied the greedy desires of the (I dare not say Christian) Spaniards. One of these Sacrilegious Robbers was John Garcia by name, who being very sick and at the point of dath, had several Idols hid under his Bed, and calling his Indians that waited on him, as a Nurse, commanded her not to part with those Idols at a small rate for they were of the better sort, and that she should not dispose of them without one Indian, for each Idol by way of Barter. Thus by this his private and Nuncupative last Will and Testament distracted with these carking cares, he gave up the Ghost: And who is it that will not fear his being tormented in the darkest and lowest Hell? Let us now consider what progress in Religion the Spaniards made, and what examples of Christianism they gave, at their first arrival in America, how devoutly they honoured God, and what expence of sweat and toil they were at to promote his Worship and Adoration among the Infidels. Let it be also taken into serious consideration, whose sin is the greater, either Joroboam's, who made all Israel to sin, and caused two Golden Calves to be erected, or the Spaniards who traffick and Trade in Idols like Judas, who was the occasion of such great scandals. These are the good Deeds of the Spanish Dons, who often, nay very often to feed their Avarice, and accumulate Gold have sold and still do sell, denied and still do deny Jesus Christ our Redeemer.

The Indians now findint the Promises of the Religious, that the Spaniards should not enter into this Countrey, null and void; nay that the Spaniards brought Idols from other places to be put off there; when as they had delivered up their own to the Priests to be burnt, that there might be only Worship of the true God established among them; they were highly incensed against these Friars, and addressed themselves to them in these Words following: Why have you deceived us, binding your promises with false protestations, that the Spaniards shoudl not be admitted to come hither? And why have you burnt our Gods, when others are brought from other Regions by the Spaniards? Are the Gods of other Provinces more sacred than ours? The Friers as well as they could (though they had little to return in answer) endevour'd by soft Language to appease them; and went to these Thirty Spaniards, declaring the evil actions they were guilty of, humbly supplicating them to withdraw themselves from that place. Which they would by no means condescend to, and what is most flagitious and wicked perswaded the Indians, that they were introduc'd by those Priests; Which being made known to them, These Indians resolved to be the death of these Monks, but having notice thereof by some courteous Indians, they stole away from thence by night, and fled; but after their departure the truth of the matter and the Spanish Malice being understood; they sent several Messengers who followed them fifty Miles distant beseeching them in the name of the Indians, to return and begging pardon for that ignorant mistake.

The Priests relying on their words, returned, and were caress'd like Angels sent from Heaven; and continued with them, (from whom they received a Thousand kindnesses) four or five months. But when the Spaniards persisted in their resolution not to quit the place, although they Vice-Roy did use all endeavours and fair means to recall them, they were Proclaim'd Traitors, guilty of High Treason; and because they continued still exercising Tyranny and perpetrated nefandous Crimes, the Priests were sensible they would study revenge, though it might be some considerable time before they put it in execution, fearing that it might fail upon their own heads, and since they could not exercise the function of their Ministry securely and undisturbed by reason of the continual Incursions and Assaults made by the Spaniards, they consulted about their departure, and did leave this Kingdom accordingly which remain'd destitute of all Christian Doctrin and these poor Souls are at this day involv'd in the obscurity of their former Misery and Ignorance, they being deprived by these accursed Spaniards, of all hopes of remedy, and the irrigatioon of Divine knowledge, just like young withering Plants for want of Water: for in that very juncture of time, when these Religioso's took leave, they embraced the Doctrine of our Faith with the greatest Fervency and Eagerness imaginable.

Of the Province of St. Martha

The Province of St. Martha was rich in the Neighbouring Golden Mines, and a fruitful Soil, nay the People were very expert and industrious in those Mine-works: Upon this Account, or Temptation it was, that from the Year 1540, to 1542, abundance of Tyrants sailed thither, laying waste the whole Country by their Depredations, slaughtering the Inhabitants at a prodigious and bloody rate; and robbing them of all their Gold, who dayly fled to their Ships for Refuge, moving sometime to one place, and sometime to another. And thus those Provinces were laid waste, the greatest Outrages being committed on the Sea-shore, which lasted till the Year 1523, whither the Spaniards then came to seat themselves, and fis their intended Habitation. And becuase it is a plentiful Region and Opulent withal; it was subjected to several Rulers, who like Infernal Fiends contended who should obtain the Palm, by out-staining the Sword of his Predecessor in Innocent Blood; insomuch, that from the Year 1529 to this very day, they have wasted and spoiled as much good ground as extended Five Hundred Miles, and unpeopled the Countrey.

If I design'd to enumerate all the Impieties, Butcheries, Desolations, Iniquities, Violences, Destructions and other the Piacula and black Enormities committed and perpetrated by the Spaniards in this Province, against God, the King, and these harmless Nations; I might compile a Voluminous History, and that shall be compleated, if God permit my Glass to run longer, in his good time. It may suffice for the present to relate some passages written in a Letter to our King and Lord by a Revernd Bishop of these Provinces, Dated the 20th of May, An. Dom. 1541. wherein among other matters he thus words it.

I must acquaint your Sacred Majesty, that the only way to succour and support this tottering Region is to free it from the Power of a Father in Law, and marry it to a Husband who will treat her as she ought to be, and lovingly entertain her, and that must be done with all possible Expedition too, if not, I am certain that she will suddenly decay and come to nothing by the covetous and sordid Deportment of the Governours, &c. And a little after he writes thus, By this Means your Majesty will plainly know and understand how to depose the Prefects or Governours of those Regions from their Office if they deserve it, that so they may be alleviated and eas'd of such Burthens; which if not perform'd, in my Opinion, the Body Politick will never recover its Health. And this I will make appear to your Majesty that they are not Christians, but Devils; not Servants of God and the King, but Traitors to the King and Laws, who are Conversant in those Regions. And in reality nothing can be more obstructive to those that live peacably, then Inhumane and Barbarous Usage, which they, who lead a quiet and peacable Life, too frequently undergo, and this is so fastidious and nauseous to them, that there can be nothing in the World so odious and detestable among them, as the Name of a Christian: for they term the Christians in their Language Yares, that is, Devils; and in truth are not without reason; for the Actions of those that reside in these Regions, are not such as speak them to be Christians or Men, gifted with Reason, but absolute Devils; hence it is, that the Indians, perceiving these Actions committed by the Heads as well as Members, who are void of all Compassion and Humanity, do judge the Christian Laws to be of the same strain and temper, and that their God and King are the Authors of such Enormities: Now to endeavour to work upon them a contrary perswasion is to no purpose; for this would afford them a greater Latitude and Liberty to deride Jesus Christ and his Laws. Now the Indians who protect and defend themselves by force of Arms, think it more eligible, and far better to dye once, than suffer several and many Deaths under the Spanish Power. This I know experimentally, Most Invicible Casar, &c. And he adds farther, Your Majesty is more Powerful in Subjects and Servants, who frequent these Kingdoms, then you can imagin. Nor is there one Soldier among them all, who does not publickly and openly profess, if he robs, steals, spoils, kills, burns His Majesties Subjects, 'tis to purchase Gold: He will not say that he therein does your Majesty great Service, for they affirm they do it to obtain their own Share and Dividend. Wherefore, Most Invincible Casar, it would be a very prudential Act for your Majesty to testifie by a rigid Correction and severe Punishment of some Malefactors, that it is disservice to you for your Subjects to commit such Evil Acts, as tend to the Disobedience and Dishonour of the Almighty.

What you have read hitherto is the Relation of the said Bishop of St. Martha, Epitomized and Extracted from his Letters, whereby it is manifest, how Savagely they handle these mild and affable People. They term them Warlike Indians, who betake themselves to the Mountains to secure themselves from Spanish Cruelty; and call them Country Indians, or Inhabitants, who by a dreadful Massacre are delivered up to Tyrannical and Horrible Servitude, whereby at length they are become depopulated, made desolate, and utterly destroy'd; as appears by the Epistle of the praementioned Bishop, who only gives us a slight Account or Essay of their persecution and Sufferings. The Indians of this Country use to break out into such Words as these, when they are driven, loaded like Brutes through the uncouth wayes in their Journeys over the Mountains, if they happen to faint through Weakness, and miscarry through extremity of Labour, (for then they are kicked and cudge'd, their Teeth dasht out with the Pummels of their Swords to raise them up again, when tired and fallen under weighty Burthens, and force them to go on without Respiration, or Time to take Breath, and all this with the following increpation, or upbraiding and taunting words, O what a wicket Villain art thou?) I say they burst out into these Expressions, I am absolutely tir'd, kill me, I desire to dye, being weary of my Life as well as my Burthen and Journey: And this not without deep Heart-breaking Sighs, they being scarce able to draw or breathe out their words, which are the Characteristical Notes, and infallible of the Mind drowned in Anguish and Sorrow. My it please our Merciful

God to order the discovery of these Crimes to be manifested to those Persons, who are able and oblig'd to redress them.

Of the Province of Carthagena

This Province is distant Fifty Miles from the Isle of St. Martha Westward, and situated on the Confines of the Country of Cenusia, from whence it extends One Hundred Miles to the Bay of Uraba, and contains a very long Tract of Land Southward. These Provinces from the Year 1498 to this present time were most barbarously us'd, and made desert by Murder and Slaughter, but that I may the sooner conclude this brief summary. I will not handle the particulars, to the end I may the better give an Account of the detestable Villanies that ruin'd other Regions.

Of the Pearl-Coast, Paria, and Trinity-Isle

The Spaniards made great Spoils and Havock from the Parian Coast to the Bay of Venecuola, exclusively, which is about Two Hundred Miles. It can hardly be exprest by Tongue or Pen how many, and how great Injuries and Injustices, the Inhabitants of this Sea-shore have endur'd from the year 1510, to this day. I will only relate Two or Three Piacular and Criminal Acts of the First Magnitude, capable of comprehending all other Enormities that deserve the sharpest Torments, Wit and Malice can invent, and so make way for a deserved Judgment upon them.

A Nameless Pirate of the Year 1510, accompanied with a parcel of Sixty or Seventy, arriv'd at Trinity-Island, which exceeds Sicile, both in Amplitude and Fertility, and is contiguous to the Continent on that side where it toucheth upon Paria, whose Inhabitants, according to their Quality, are more addicted to Probity and Vertue, than the rest of the Indians; who immediately published an Edict, that all the Inhabitants should come and cohabit with them. The Indian Lords and Subjects gave them a Debonair and Brotherly Reception, serving them with wonderful Alacrity, furnishing them with dayly

Provisions in so plentiful a manner, that they might have sufficed a more numerous Company; for it is the Mode among Indians of this New World, to supply the Spaniards very bountifuly with all manner of Necessaries. A short time after the Spaniards built a stately House, which was an Appartment for the Indians, that they might accomplish their praemeditated Designs, which was thus effected. When they were to thatch it, and had rais'd it two Mens height, they inclos'd several of them there, to expedite the Work, as they pretended, but in truth that they who were within, might not see those without; thus part of them surrounded the House with Sword in Hand that no one should stir out, and part of them entred it, and bound the Indians, menacing them with Death, if they offered to move a Foot; and if any one endeavoured to escape, he was presently hackt in pieces; but some of them partly wounded, and partly unwounded getting away, with others who went not into the House, about One Hundred and Two Hundred, betook themselves to another House with Bows and Arrows; and when they were all there, the Spaniards secur'd the Doors, throwing in Fire at another place, and so they all perished. From hence they set Sail to the Island of St. John with near upon One Hundred and Eighty Slaves, whom they had bound, where they sold one half of them, and thence to Hispaniola, where they dispos'd of the rest. Now when I taxed this Captain with Wickedness and Treachery in the very Isle of St. John, he dismist me with this Answer; Forbear good Sir. I had this in commission from those who sent me hither, that I should surprize them by the spetious pretense of Peace, whom I could not sieze by open Force, and in truth this same Captain told me with his own Mouth, that in Trinity-Isle alone, he had met with a Father and Mother in Civil usage, which he uttered to his greater Confusion and the aggravation of his Sins. The Monks of our Order of St. Dominic on a certain time held a Consult about sending one of their Fraternity into this Island, that by their Preaching they might instruct them in the Christian Faith, and teach them the way to be sav'd, of which they were wholly Ignorant. And to this end they sent thither a Religious and Licentiate in Theologie, (or Doctor in Divinity, as we term it among us) a Man Famous for his Vertue and Holiness with a

Laic his Associate, to visit the Country, converse with the Inhabitants, and find out the most convenient places for the Erection of Monasteries. As soon as they were arriv'd according to custom, they were entertain'd like Coelestial Messengers, with great Affection, Joy and Respect, as well as they could, for they were ignorant of their Tongue, and so made use of signs, for the present. It hapned that after the departure of that Vessel that brought these Religious Men, another came into the Port, whose Crew according to their Hellish Custom, fraudulently, and unknown to the Religious brought away a Prince of that Province as Captive, who was call'd Alphonsus, (for they are ambitious of a Christian Name,) and forthwith desire without farther Information, that he would Baptize him: But the said Lord Alphonsus was deceitfully overperswaded to go on board of them with his Wife and about Seventeen more, pretending that they would give hime a Collation; which the Prince and they did, for he was confident, that the Religious would by no means suffer himo be abus'd, for he had no so much Confidence in the Spaniards; but as soon as they were upon Deck, the perfidious Rogues, set Sail for Hispaniola, where they were sold as Slaves. The whole Country being extreamly discompos'd, and understanding that their Prince and Princess were violently carried away, addressed themselves to these Religioso's, who were in great danger of losing their Lives: But they being made to understand this unjust Action, were extraordinarily afflicted, and 'tis probable would have suffered Death, rather than permit the Indians to be so injuriously dealt with, which might prove an Obstruction to their receiving of, and believing in God's Word. Yet the Indians were sedated by the promises of the Religious; for they told them, they would send Letters by the first Ship that was bound for Hispaniola, whereby they would procure the Restitution and Return of their Lord and his Retinue. It pleased God to send a Ship thither forthwith, to the greater confirming of the Governours Damnation, where in the Letters they sent to the Religious of Hispaniola, Letters containing repeated Exclamations and Protestations, and protest against such Actions, but those that received them denied them Justice, for that they were partakers of that Prey, made of those Indians so injustly and impiously captivated. But when the Religious, who had engag'd to the Inhabitants, that their Lord Alphonsus should be restor'd within Four Moneths, and found that neither in Four, nor Eight Moneths he was return'd, they prepar'd themselves for Death, and to deliver up their Life to Christ, to whom they had offer'd it before their departure from Spain: Thus the Innocent Indians were revenged on the Innocent Priests; for they were of Opinion, that the Religious had a hand in the Plot, partly, because they found their Promises that their Lord should return within Four Moneths, ineffectual, and partly because the Inhabitants made no difference between a Religious Frier and a Spanish Rogue. At another time it fell out likewise, through the Rampant Tyrrany and Cruel Deeds of evil-minded Christians, that the Indians put to Death two Dominican Friers, of which I am a faithful Witness, escaping my self, not without a very great Miracle, which Transaction I resolve silently to pass over, lest I should terrifie the Reader with the Horror of the Fact.

In these Provinces, there was a City seated on the Bay of Codera, whose Lord was call'd Higueroto, a Name, either proper to Persons or common to the Rulers of that Place. A Cacic of such signal Clemency, and his Subjects of such noted Vertue, that the Spaniards who came thither, were extraordinarily welcom, furnished with Provisions, enjoying Peace and Comfort, and no Refreshment wanting: But a perfidious Wretch got many of them on board, and sold them to the Islanders of St. John. At the same time I landed upon that Island, where I obtained a sight of this Tyrant, and heard the Relation of his Actions. He utterly destroy'd that Land, which the rest of the Spaniards took very unkindly at his Hands, who frequently playd the Pirate, and rob'd on that shore, detesting it as a wicked thing, because they had lost that place, where they use to be treated with as great Hospitality and Freedom, as if they had been under their own Roof: Nay they transported from this place, among them, to the Isles of Hispaniola and St. John Two Millions of Men and upward, and made the Coast a Desert.

It is most certainly true, that they never ship off a Vessel freighted with Indians, but they pay a third part as Tribute to the Sea, besides those who are slaughter'd, when found in their own Houses. Now the Soarce and Original of all this is the ends they have propos'd to themselves. For there is a necessity of taking with them a great number of Indians, that they may gain a great sum of Mony by their Sale, now the Ships are very slenderly furnished with Provisions and Water in small Quantity, to satisfie few, left the Tyrants, who are term'd Owners or Proprietors of Ships should be at too great expence in Victualling their Vessels, nay they scarce carry Food enough with them to maintain the Spaniards that manage the Vessel, which is the reason so many Indians dye with Hunger and Thirst, and of necessity they must be thrown over-board: Nay one of them told me this for a Truth, that there being such a Multitude of Men thus destroy'd, a Ship may sail from the Isle of Lucaya to Hispaniola, which is a Voyage of Twenty Leagues and upward, without Chart or Compass, by the sole Direction or Observation of dead fluctuating Carkasses.

But afterward, when arriv'd, and driven up into the Isle whither they are brought to be sold, there is no Person that is in some small measure compassionate, but would be extreamly mov'd and discompos'd at the sight; viz. to spie old Men and Women, together with Naked Children half starv'd. Then they separate Parents from Children, Wives from their Husbands, about Ten or Twenty in a Company, and cast lots for them, that the Detestable Owners of the Ships may have their share; who prepare Two or Three Ships, and equip them as a Fleet of Pirates, going ashore ravaging and forcing Men out of their Houses, and then robbing them: But when the lot of any one of them falls upon a parcel, that hath an aged or diseased Man; the Tyrant, whose Allotment he is, usually bursts out, as followeth. Let this old Fellow be Damm'd, why do you bestow him upon me; must I, think you; be at the charge of his Burial? And this sickly Wretch, how comes he to be one of my alloted portion must I take care for his cure? Not I. Hence you may guess what estimate and value the Spaniards put upon Indians, and whether they practise and fulful that Divine and Heavenly precept injoyning mutual Love and Society.

There can be nothing more cruel and detestable then the Tyrannical usage of the Spaniards towards the Indians in their Pearl-Fishing; for the Torments undergone in the unnatural Exenteration and tearing out with Paracidal hands the richer bowels of our common Mother, or the inward cruciating racks of the most profligate, Heaven daring Desperado can admit of no comparison with these, although the extracting or digging for Gold is one of the sharpest subterranean Drudgeries, they plunge them down four or five ells deep under Water, where swimming about without breathing, they eradicate and pull up Oisters, wherein the Pearls are engendred. Sometimes they rise up to the superfities of the Water with Nets full of Oisters for respiration and Air, but if these miserable Creatures stay but a little more then is Ordinary to rest themselves the Hangman is immediately upon them in a Canow or small Boat, who beating them with many stripes drag them by the hair of the head under Water, that they may drudge again at their expilcation or Pearl Fishing. Their Food is Fish, and the same which contains the Pearls and Cassabus made of Roots with a few Mahids, the Bread of that Countrey; in the former there is little or no nutriment or substance, and the other is not made without great trouble, nor for all this have they a sufficient allowance thereof to support nature. Their Lodging or Bed is the Earth confined to a pair of Stocks, for fear that they should run away: And it frequently happens that they are drown'd with the toil of this kind of Fishing and never more seen, for the Tuberoms and Maroxi (certain Marine Monsters that devour a complete proportioned Man wholly at once) prey upon them under Water. You must consider withall, that it is impossible for the strongest constitution to continue long under Water without breathing, and they ordinarily dye through the extream rigor of the Cold, spitting Blood which is occasioned by the too great compression of the Breast, procreated by a continued holding breath under Water, for by too much cold a profluvium of blood follows. Their hair naturally black is changed into a combust, burnt or Suncolour like that of the Sea Wolves, their shoulders and backs covered, or overspread with a saltish humor that they appear rather like Monsters in humane shape then Men.

They have destroy'd all the Lucayans by this intolerable or rather Diabolical exercise, for the accustomary emolument or gain of lucre, and by this means gain'd the value of fifty, sometime one hundred Crowns of every individual Indian. They sell them (though it is prohibited) publickly; for the Lucayans were excellent Swimmers, and several perished in this Isle that came from other Provinces.

Of the River Yuya Pari

This River washeth the Province arising from its head or fountain in another Region, Two Hundred miles off and better, By this a wretched Tyrant entred it and laid waste the Land for the space of many miles, and murder'd abundance of them by Fire and Sword, &c. At length he died violently, and all his Forces moldred away of themselves, many succeeded him in his iniquity and cruelty and so dayly destroy them, sending to Hell the Souls redeemed by the blood of the Son of God.

Of the Kingdom of Venecuela

Our Sovereign Lord the King in the Year 1526, over-perswaded by fallacious appearances (for the Spaniards use to conceal from His Majesties knowledge the dammages and detriments, which God himself, the Souls and state of the Indians did suffer) intrusted the Kingdom of Venecuela longer and larger then the Spanish Dominions, with its Government and absolute Jurisdiction to some German Merchants, with power to make certain Capitulations and Conventions, who came into this Kingdom with Three Hundred Men, and there found a benign mild and peaceable people, as they were throughout the Indies till injured by the Spaniards. These more cruel then the rest beyond comparison, behav'd themselves more inhumanely then rapacious Tygres Wolves and Lyons, for they had the jurisdiction of this Kingdom, and therefore possessing it with the greater freedom from controul; lay in wait and were the more vigilant with greater care and avarice to understand the practical part of heaping up Wealth, and robbing the Inhabitants of their Gold and Sliver, surpassing all their Predecessors in those indirect ways, rejecting wholly both the fear of their God and King, nay forgetting that they were born men with reasonable Faculties.

These incarnate Devils laid waste and desolate Four Hundred miles of most Fertile Land, containing vast and wonderful Provinces, most spatious and large Valleys surrounded with Hills, forty Miles in Length, and many Towns richly abounding in Gold and Silver. They destroy'd so many and such considerable Regions, that there is not one supernumerary witness left to relate the Story, unless perchance some that lurkt in the Caverns and Womb of the Earth to evade death by their inhumane Swords embrew'd in Innocent Indian blood, escaped. I judge that they by new invented and unusual Torments ruinated four or five Millions of Souls and sent them all to Hell. I will give a taste of two or three of their Transactions, that hereby you may guess at the rest.

They made the supream Lord of the Province a Slave, to squeeze his Gold from him, racking him to extort his confession who escaping fled into the Mountains, their common Sanctuary, and his Subjects lying absconded in the Thickets of the Woods, were stir'd up to Sedition and Tumult or Mutiny. The Spaniards follow and destroy many of them, but those that were taken alive and in their power were all publickly sold for Slaves by the Common Crier.

They were in all Provinces they came into entertained and welcomed by the Indians with Songs, Dances and Rich Presents but Rewarded very ungratefully with bloodshed and Slaughter. The German Captain and Tyrant caused several of them to be clapt into a Thatcht House, and there cut in pieces; but some of them to avoid falling by their bloody and merciless Swords, climb'd up to the beams and Rafters of the House, and the Governour, hearing it (O cruel Brute?) commanded Fire to be put to it and burnt them all alive, leaving the Region desert and desolate.

They also came to another stately Province, bordering on St. Martha; whose inhabitants did them many egregious and notable services, bestowing on them innumerable quantities of Gold besides many other gifts, but when they were upon departure, in retribution of their Civil Treating and Deportment the German Tyrant, commanded that all the Indians, with their Wives and Children if possible, should be taken into Custody; inclosed in some large capacious place, and that there it should be signified unto them, whosoever desired to be set at Liberty should redeem himself at the Will and Pleasure (as to price;) of the unjust Governour, or at a certain rate imposed upon himself, his wife and every Childs head; and to expedite the business prohibited the administration or allowance of any food to them, till the Gold required for Redemption was paid down to the utmost grain. Several of them sent home to discharge the demanded price of their Redemption, and procur'd their Freedom, as well as they could by one means or other, that so they might return to their Livelihood and profession, but not long after he sent other Rogues and Robbers among them to enslave those that were Redeemed.

To the same Gaol they are brought a second time, being instigated or rather constrained to a speedy Redemption by hunger and thirst; Thus many of them were twice or thrice taken, captiv'd and Redeedmed; but some who were not capable of Depositing such a sum, perished there. Farthermore this Tyrant was big with an itching desire after the discovery of the Perusian Mines, which he did accomplish. Nay should I enumerate the particular Cruelties, Slaughters, &c. committed by him though my discourse would not in the least be contrariant to the Truth, yet it would not be beleived and only stupifie and amaze the Reader.

This course the other Tyrants took who set sail from Venecuela and St. Martha (with the same Resolution of detecting the Perusian

Golden, Consecrated Houses as them they esteemed) who found the fruitful Region so desolate, deserted, and wasted by Fire and Sword, that those Cruel Tyrants themselves were smitten with wonder and astonishment at the traces and ruins of such prodigious Devastations.

All these things and many more were prov'd by Witness in the Indian Exchequer, and the Records of their Testimony were entred in that Court, though these execrable Tyrants burnt many of them that there might be little or nothing prov'd as a cause of those great Devastations and Evils perpetrated by them. For the Minister of Justice who have hitherto lived in India, through their obscure and damnable blindness, were not much sollicitous about the punishment of the Crimes and Butcheries which have been and are still committed by these Tyrants, only they may say possibly because such a one, and such a one hath wickedly and barbarously dealt with the Indians, that is the reason so great a summ of Crowns in Money is diminished already or retrenched from His Majesties Annual Revenue, and this general and confused proof is sufficient (as they worthily conceive) to purge or repress such great and hainous Crimes. And though they are but few, are not verified as they ought to be, nor do they attribute and lay upon them that stress and weight as they ought to do, for if they did perform their Duty to God and the King; it could not be made apparent as it may be, that these German Tyrants have cheated and rob'd the King of Three Millions of Gold and upward; and thus these Enemies to God and the King began to depopulate these Regions and destroy them, cheating his Majesty of Two Millions of Gold per Annum, nor can it be expected, that the Detriment done to his Majesty can possibly be retriev'd, as long as the Sun and moon endures, unless God by a Miracle should raise as many Thousands from Death to Life, as have bin destroy'd. And these are the Temporal Dammages the King suffers. It would be also a Work worthy the inquiry into, to consider how many cursed Sacriledges and Indignities God himself hath been affronted with to the dishonour of his Name. And what Recompence can be made for the loss of so many Souls as are now tormented in Hell by the

Cruelty and Covetousness of these Brutish German Tyrants. But I will conclude all their Impiety and Barbarisme with one Example, viz. That from the time they entred upon this Country to this very day, that is, Seventeen Years, they have remitted many Ships fraighted with Indians to be sold as Slaves to the Isles of St. Martha, Hispaniola, Jamaica, and St. John, selling a Million of Persons at the least, I speak modestly, and still do expose to Sale to this very Year of our Lord 1542, the King's Council in this Island seeing and knowing it, yet what they find to be manifest and apparent they connive at, permit and countenance, and wink at the horrid Impieties and Devastations innumerable which are committed on the Coasts of this Continent, extending Four Hundred Miles in Length, and continues still together with Venecuela and St. Martha under their Jurisdiction, which they might easily have remedied and timely prevented.

Of the Provinces of Florida

Three Tyrants at several times made their entrance into these Provinces since the Year 1510, or 1511, to act those Crimes which others, and two of these Three made it their sole business to do in other Regions, to the end, that they might advance themselves to higher Dignities and Promotions than they could deserve, by the Effusion of Blood and Destruction of these People; but at length they all were cut off by a violent Death, and the Houses which they formerly built and erected with the cement of Human Blood, (which I can sufficiently testifie of these three) perished with them, and their memory roten, and as absolutely washed away from off the Face of the Earth, as if they had never had a being. These Men deserted these Regions, leaving them in great distraction and confusion, nor were they branded with less notes of infamy, by the certain Slaughters they perpetrated, though they were but few in number than the rest. For the Just God cut them off before they did much Mischief, and reserv'd the Castigation and Revenge of those Evils which I know, and was an Eye-Witness of, to this very Time and Place. As to the Fourth Tyrant, who lately, that is, in the Year

1538, came hither well-furnished with Men and Ammunition, we have received no account these Three Years last past; but wer are very confident, that he, at his first Arrival, acted like a bloody Tyrant, even to extasie and madness, if he be still alive with his Follower, and did injure, destroy, and consume a vast Number of Men (for he was branded with infamous Cruelty above all those who with their Assistants committed Crimes and Enormities of the first Magnitude in these Kingdoms and Provinces) I conceive, God hath punished him with the same Violent Death, as he did other Tyrants: But because my Pen is wearied with relating such Execrable and Sanguinary Deeds (not of Men but Beasts) I will trouble my self no longer with the dismal and fatal Consequences thereof.

These People were found by them to be Wise, Grave, and well dispos'd, though their usual Butcheries and Cruelties in opressing them like Brutes, with heavy Burthens, did rack their minds with great Terror and Anguish. At their Entry into a certain Village, they were welcomed with great Joy and Exultation, replenished them with Victuals, till they were all satisfied, yielding up to them above Six Hundred Men to carry their Bag and Baggage, and like Grooms to look after their Horses: The Spaniards departing thence, a Captain related to the Superiour Tyrant returned thither to rob this (no ways diffident or mistrustful) People, and pierced their King through with a Lance, of which Wound he dyed upon the Spot, and committed several other Cruelties into the bargain. In another Neighboring Town, whose Inhabitants they thought, were more vigilant and watchful, having had the News of their horrid Acts and Deeds, they barbarously murdered them all with their Lances and Swords, destroying all, Young and Old, Great and Small, Lords and Subject without exception.

The Chief Tyrant caused many Indians (above Two Hundred as 'tis noised abroad) whom he summon'd to appear before him out of another town, or else, who came voluntarily to pay their Respects to him, to have their Noses and Lips to the very Beard, cut off; and thus in this grievous and wretched Condition, the Blood gushing out of their Wounds, return'd them back, to give an Infallible Testimony of the Works and Miracles wrought by these Preachers and Ministers baptized in the Catholick Faith.

Now let all Men judge what Affection and love they bear to Christianity; to what purpose, or upon what account they believe there is a God, whom they preach and boast of to be Good and Just, and that his Law which they profess (and indeed only profess) to be pure and immaculate. The Mischiefs acted by these profligate Wretches and Sons of Perdition were of the deepest die. At last this Captain devoted to Perdition dyed impenitent, nor do we in the least question, but that he is overwhelmed and buried in Darkness Infernal, unless God according to his Infinite Mercy and boundless Clemency, not his own Merits, (he being contaminated and poison'd with Execrable Deeds,) be pleas'd to compassionate and have Mercy upon him.

Of the Plate-River, that is, the Silver-River

Some Captains since the Year 1502 to 1503 undertook Four or Five Voyages to the River of Plate, which embraceth within its own Arms great Kingdoms and Provinces, and is peopled by rational and well-temper'd Inhabitants. In the general we are certified, that they were very injurious and bloody to them; but they being far distant from those Indians, we frequently discourse of, wer are not able to give you a particular account of their Transactions. Yet beyond all Controversie, they did, and still do go the same way to work, as others in several Regions to this present time do, and have done; for they are the same, (and many in number too) Spaniards who went thither, that were the wicked Instruments of other Executions, and all of them aim at one and the same thing, namely to grow Rich and Wealthy, which they can never be, unless they steer the same Course which others have followed, and tread the same paths in Murdering, Robbing and Destroying poor Indians.

After I had committed to Writing what I have prementioned, it was told me for a great Truth, that they had laid waste in those Countreys great Kingdoms and Provinces, dealing Cruelly and Bloodily with these harmless People, at a horrid rate, having a greater Opportunity and Convenience to be more Infamous and Rigid to them, then others, they being very remote from Spain, living inordinatly, like Debauches, laying aside, and bidding farewel to all manner of Justice, which is indeed a Stranger in all the American Regions, as is manifest by what hath been said already. But among the other Numerous Wicked Acts following this is one that may be read in the Indians Courts. One of the Governours commanded his Soldiers to go to a certain Village, and if they denyed them Provisions, to put all the Inhabitants to the Sword: By Vertue of this Authority away they march, and because they would not yield to them above Five Thousand Men as Enemies, fearing rather to be seen, then guilty of Illiberality, were cut off by the Sword. Also a certain number of Men living in Peace and Tranquillity proffered their services to him; who, as it fell out, were call'd before the Governour, but deferring their appearance a little longer than ordinary, that he might infix their minds with a remark of horrible Tyranny, he commanded, they should be deliver'd up, as Prisoners to their Mortal Indian Enemies, who beg'd with loud Clamours and a Deluge of Tears, that they might be dispatcht out of this World by their own Hands, rather than be given up as a prety to the Enemy; yet being resolute, they would not depart out of the House wherein they were, so the Spaniards hackt them in pieces Limb by Limb, who exclaim'd and cryed aloud, "We came to visit and serve you peaceably and quietly, and you Murder us; our Blood with which these Walls are moistned and sprinkled will remain as an Everlasting Testimony of our Unjust Slaughter, and your Barbarous Cruelty. And really this Piaculum or horrid Crime deserves a Commemoration, or rather speak more properly, the Commiseration of all Persons."

Of the vast Kingdoms and Spatious Provinces of Perusia

A notorious Tyrant in the Year 1531, entred the Kingdoms of Perusia with his Complices, upon the same Account, and with the same pretences, and beginning at the same Rate as others did; he indeed being one of those who were exercised, and highly concern'd in the Slaughters and Cruelties committed on the Continent ever since the Year 1510, he increased and heightned the Cruelties, Butcheries, and Rapine; destroying and laying waste (being a False-hearted Faithless Person) the Towns and Villages, and Murdering the Inhabitants, which occasion'd all those Evils, that succeeded in those Regions afterward: Now to undertake the Writing of a Narrative of them, and represent them lively and Naturally to the Readers view, and perusal, is a work altogether impossible, but must lie concealed and unknown until they shall more openly and clearly appear, and be made visible to every Eye, at the day of Judgement. As for my part, if I should presume to unravel, in some, measure the Deformity, Quality and Circumstances of those Enormities, I must ingenuously confess I could by no means perform so burthensom a Task, and render it compleat and as it ought to be.

At his first admission into these parts, he had laid waste some Towers, and rob'd them of a great quantity of Gold, this he did in the Infancy of his Tyrannical Attempts, when he arriv'd at Pugna a Neighbouring Isle so called, he had the Reception of an Angel; but about Six Months after, when the Spaniards had spent all their Provisions, they discover'd and opened the Indians Stores and Granaries, which were laid up for the sustenance of themselves, Wives and Children against a time of Dearth and Scarcity, brought them forth with Tears and Weepings, to dispose of at pleasure: But they rewarded them with Slaughter, Slavery and Depopulation as formerly.

Thence they betook themselves to the Isle Tumbala, scituate on the firm Land, where they put to Death all they met with. And because the People terrified with their abominable Sins of Commission, fled from their Cruelty, they were accused of Rebellion against the Spanish King. This Tyrant made use of this Artifice, he commanded all that he took, or that had bestowed Gold, Silver and other rich Gifts on him, still to load him with other Presents, till he found they had exhausted their Treasures, and were grown naked and incapable of affording him farther supplies, and then he declared them to be the Vassals and Subjects of the King of Spain, flattering them, and proclaiming twice by sound of Trumpet, that for the future he would not captivate or molest them any more, looking upon it as lawful to rob, and terrifie them with such Messages as he had done, before he admited them under the King's protection, as if from that very time, he had never rob'd, destroy'd or opprest them with Tyrannical Usage.

Not long after Ataliba the King and Supreme Emperor of all these Kingdoms, leading a great Number of Naked Men, he himself being at the Head of them, armed with ridiculous Weapons, and wholly ignorant of the goodness of the Spaniards Bilbo-Blades, the Mortal Dartings of their Lances, and the Strength of their Horse, whose Use and Service was to him altogether unknown, and never so much as heard of before, and that the Spaniards were sufficiently weapon'd to rob the Devils themselves of Gold, if they had any, came to the place where they then were; saying, Where are these Spaniards? Let them appear, I will not stir a foot from hence till they give me satisfaction for my Subjects whom they have slain, my Towns they have reduc'd to Ashes, and my Riches they have stoln from me. The Spaniards meet him, make a great Slaughter of his Men, and seize on the Person of the King Himself, who was carried in a Chair or Sedan on Mens Shoulders. There was a Treaty had about his Redemption, the King engaged to lay down Four Millions of Crowns, as the purchase of his Freedom, but Fifteen were paid down upon the Nail: They promise to set him at Liberty, but contrary to all Faith and Truth according to their common Custom (for they always violated their promises with the Indians) they falsly imposed this upon him, that his People were got together in a Body by his Command; but the King was made answer, That throughout his Dominions, not so much as a Leaf upon a Tree durst move without his Authority and Pleasure, and if any were assembled together, they must of necessity believe that it was done without his Order, he being a Captive, it being in their power to deprive him of his LIfe, if any such thing should be ordered by him: Notwithstanding which, they entred into a Consultation to have him burnt alive, and a little while after the Sentence was agreed upon, but the Captain at the intreaty of some Persons commanded him first to be strangled, and afterward thrown into the fire. The King understanding the sentence of Death past upon him, said; Why do you burn me? What Fact have I committed deserving Death? Did you not promise to set me free for a Sum of Gold. And did I not give you a far larger quantity than I promised? But if it is your pleasure so to do, send me to your King of Spain, and thus using many words to the same purpose, tending to the Confusion and Detestation of the Spanish Injustice, he was burnt to Death. And here let us take into serious Consideration the Right and Title they had to make this War, the Captivity, Sentence, and Execution of this Prince, and the Conscience wherewith these Tyrants have possessed themselves of vast Treasures, which they have surreptitiously and fraudulently taken away from this King, and a great many more of the Rulers of these Kingdoms. But as to the great number of their Enormities committed by those who stile themselves Christians in order to the extirpation of this People, I will hear repeat some of them, which in the very beginning were seen by a Franciscan, confirm'd by his own Letters, and signed with his Hand and Seal, sending some of them to the Perusian Provinces, and others to the Kingdom of Castile: A Copy whereof I have in my Custody, Signed with his Hand, as I said before; the Contents whereof follow.

I Frier Marcus de Xlicia, of the Franciscan Order, and Praefect of the whole Fraternity residing in the Perusian Provinces, one of the first among the Religious, who arriv'd with the Spaniards in these parts. I decalre with incontrovertible and undeniable Testimony, those Transactions, which I saw with my own Eyes, and particularly such as relate to the usage of the Inhabitants of this Region. In the first place I was an Eye-Witness, and am certainly assur'd, that these Perusians are a People, who transcend all other Indians in Meekness, Clemency, and Love to Spaniards; and I have seen the Indians bestow very liberally on them Gold, Silver, and Jewels, being very serviceable to them many other wayes. Nor did the Indians ever betake themselves to their Arms in an Hostile manner, till by infinite Injuries and Cruelties they were compell'd thereunto: For on the contrary, they gave the Spaniards an amicable and honourable Reception in all their Towns, and furnished them with Provisions, and as many Male and Female Servants as they required.

I can also farther testifie, that the Spaniards, without the least provocation on their part, as soon as they entred upon these Territories, did burn at the Stake their most Potent Caciq Ataliba, Prince of the whole Country, after they had extorted from him above Two Millions of Gold, and possessed themselves of his Province, without the least Opposition: and Cochilimaca, his Captain General, who with other Rulers, came peaceably into them, follow'd him by the same fiery Tryal and Death. As also some few days after, the Ruler of the Province of Quitonia, who was burnt, without any Cause given, or Crime laid to his Charge. They likewise put Schapera, Prince of the Canaries to the same Death, and in like manner, burnt the Feet of Alvidis, the greatest of all the Quitonian Lords, and rackt him with other Torments to Extract from him a discovery of Ataliba's Treasure, whereof as appear'd after, he was totally ignorant. Thus they treated Cocopaganga, Governour of all the Provinces of Quitonia, who being overcome with the Intreaties of Sebastian Bernalcarus, the Governours Captain, went peaceably to pay them a Visit; but because he could not give them as much Gold as they demanded, they burnt him with many other Casics and Chief Persons of Quality. And as I understnad, did it with this evil Intention, that they might not leave one surviving Lord or Peer in the whole Countrey.

I also affirm that I saw with these Eyes of mine the Spaniards for no other reason, but only to gratifie their bloody mindedness, cut off the Hands, Noses, and Ears, both of Indians and Indianesses, and that in so many places and parts, that it would be too prolix and tedious to relate them. Nay, I have seen the Spaniards let loose their Dogs upon the Indians to bait and tear them in pieces, and such a Number of Villages burnt by them as cannot well be discover'd: Farther this is a certain Truth, that they snatched Babes from the Mothers Embraces, and taking hold of their Arms threw them away as far as they would from them: (a pretty kind of barr-tossing Recreation.) They committed many other Cruelties, which shook me with Terror at the very sight of them, and would take up too much time in the Relation.

I likewise aver, That the Spaniards gathered together as many Indians as fill'd Three Houses, to which, for no cause, (or a very inconsiderable one) they set fire, and burnt every one of them: But a Presbyter, Ocana by Name, chanced to snatch a little baby out of the fire, which being observ'd by a Spaniard, he tore him out of his Arms, and threw him into the midst of the Flames, where he was with the rest, soon burnt to Ashes, which Spaniard the same day he committed that Fact, returning to his Quarters, dyed suddenly by the way, and I advised them not to give him Christian Burial.

Farthermore I saw them send to several Casics and Principal Indians, promising them a protecting Passeport to travel peaceably and securely to them, who, no sooner came, but they were burnt; Two of them before my Face, one at Andonia, and the other at Tumbala, nor could I with all my perswasions and preaching to them prevail so far as to save them from the Fire. And this I do maintain according to God and my own Conscience, as far as I could possibly learn, that the Inhabitants of Perusia never promoted or raised any Commotion or Rebellion, though as it is manifest to all Men, they were afflicted with Evil Dealings and Cruel Torments: And they, not without Cause, the Spaniards breaking their Faith and Word, betraying the Truth and Tyrannically contrary to all Law and Justice, destroying them and the whole Country, inflicting on them great Injuries and Losses, were more reay to prepare themselves for Death, than still to fall at once into such great and irrecoverable Miseries.

Nay I do declare, according to Information from the Indians themselves, that there are to this day far greater Quantities of Gold kept hid and concealed than ever were yet detected or brought to light, which by means of the Spanish Injustice and Cruelty, they would not then, nor ever will discover so long as they are so barbarously treated, but will rather chose to dye with the Herd. Whereat the Lord God is highly offended and the King hath very ill Offices done him, for he is hereby defrauded of this Region, which was sufficiently able to furnish all Castile with Necessaries, the Recovery whereof can never be expected without great difficulty and vast Expenses.

Thus far I have acquainted you with the very words of this Religious Franciscan, ratified by the Bishop of Mexico, who testifieth that the said Frier Marc did affirm and maintain what is above-mentioned.

Here it is to be observ'd what this said Frier was an Eye-Witness of; for he travelled up in this Countrey Fifty or a Hundred Miles, for the space of Nine or Ten Years, when as yet, few Spaniards had got footing there, but afterward, at the noise of Gold to be had there in great plenty, Four or Five Thousand came thither, who spread themselves through those Kingdoms and Provinces the space of Five or Six Hundred Miles, which they made wholly desloate, committing the same, or greater Cruelies than are before recited; for in reality they destroyed from that time to these very days, above an Hundred Thousand poor Souls more than he gives an Account of, and with less fear of God and the King, nay with less Mercy have they destroyed the greatest part of Mankind in these Kingdoms, above Four Millions suffering by violent Death.

A few days after they darted to Death with Arrows made of Reeds a Puissant Queen, the Wife of a Potentate, who still sways the Imperial Scepter of that Kingdom, whom the Spaniards had a design to take, which instigated him to raise a Rebellion, and he still continues a Rebel. They seized the Queen his Consort, and contrary to all Law and Equity murdered her, as is said before, who was then, as report, big with Child, only for this Reason, that they might add fresh Affliction and Grief to her Husband.

Of the New Kingdom of Granada

Many Tyrants there were, who set Sail from Venecuela, St. Martha, and Carthagena, hastening to the Conquest of Perusia, Anno Dom. 1539. and they accompanied with many more going farther from this Region, endeavored to penetrate into the Heart of this Countrey, where they found about Three Hundred Miles from Carthagena and St. Martha, many admirable Provinces and most fruitful Land, furnished with an even-tempered or meek-spirited People, as they are in other parts of India; very rich in Gold and those sorts of precious Stones known by the name of Emralds: To which Province they gave the Name of Granada, upon this account, because the Tyrant who first arrived in these Regions, was born in the Kingdom of Granada belonging to these parts; now they that spoiled these Provinces with their rapine being wicked, cruel, infamous Butchers, and delighting in the effusion of Humane Blood, having practically experimented the piacular and grand Enormities perpetrated among the Indians; and upon this account their Diabolical Actions are so great, so many in number, and represented so grievously horrid by circumstantial aggravations, that they exceed all the villanies committed by others, nay by themselves in other Regions, I will only select and cull out a few out of so great a number which have bene transacted by them within these three years, for my present purpose.

A certain Governour, because he that went to commit depredations and spoils in the Kingdom of Granada, would not admit him, as a

Companion in his Robberies and Cruelties, set up an Inquisition, and produced proofs confirmed by great evidence, whereby he palpably lays open, and proves the Slaughters and Homicides he committed, and persists in to this very day, which were read in the Indian Courts of Judicature, and are there now Recorded.

In this Inquisition the Witnesses depose, that when all these Kingdoms enjoy'd Peace and Tranquillity, the Indians serv'd the Spaniards, and got their living by contstnat day-labour in Tilling and Manuring the Ground, bringing them much Gold, and many Gems, particularly Emeralds, and what other Commodities they could, and possessed, their Cities and Dominions being divided among the Spaniards, to procure which is the chiefest of their care and pains; and these are the proper measures they take to obtain their proposed ends, to wit, heaping and treasuring up of Gold and Riches.

Now when all the Indians were under their accustomed Tyranny: A certain Tyrant, and Chief Commander, took the King and Lord of the whole Countrey, and detain'd him Captive for six or seven moneths, demanding of him, without any reason, store of Gold and Emeralds. The said King, whose name was Bogoca, though fear, promised him a House of Gold, hoping, in time, to escape out of his clutches, who thus plagu'd him, and sent some Indians for Gold, who frequently, and at several times, brought him a great quantity of Gold, and many Jewels; but because the King did not, according to his promise, bestow upon him an Apartment made of pure Gold, he must therefore forfeit his Life. The Tyrant commanded himto be brought to Tryal before himself, and so they cite and summon to a Tryal the greatest King in the whole Region; and the Tyrant pronounced this Sentence, that unless he did perform his Golden Promise he should be exposed to severe Torments. They rackt him, poured boiling Soap into his Bowels, chain'd his Legs to one post, and fastened his Neck to another, two men holding his Hands, and so applyed the scorching heat of the Fire to his Feet; the Tyrant himself often casting his eye upon him, and threatning him with death, if he did not give him the promised Gold; and thus with these kind of horrid torments, the said Lord was destroy'd; which while they were doing, God being willing to manifest how displeasing these Cruelties are to His Divine Majesty, the whole City, that was the Stage on which they were acted, was consumed by fire; and the rest of the Captains following his example, destroy'd all the Lords of that Region by Fire and Faggot.

Once it fell out, that many Indians addressed themselves to the Spaniards with all Humility and Simplicity, as they use to do, who thinking themselves safe and secure, behold the Captain comes into the City, where they were to do their work, and commands all these Indians, sleeping and taking their rest, after Supper, being wearied with the heavy drudgery of the day, to be slain by the Sword: And this stratagem he put in practice, to make a greater impression of fear on all the minds of the Inhabitants; and another time a certain Captain commanded the Spaniards to declare upon Oath, how many Casics and Indians every individual person had in his Family at home, who were presently lead to a publick place, and lost their Heads; so there perisht, that bout, four or five hundred Men. The Witnesses depose this of a particular Tyrant, that by beating, cutting off the Hands and Noses of many Women as well as Men, and destroying several persons in great numbers, he exercised horrid Cruelties.

Then one of the Captains sent this bloody Tyrant into the Province of Bogata, to inquire who succeeded that Prince there, whom he so barbarously and inhumanely Murder'd, who traveling many miles in this Countrey, took as many Indians as he could get, some of which, because they did not tell him who was Successor of this Deceased Prince, had their Hands cut off, and others were exposed to hunger-starv'd Currs, to be devour'd by them, and as many of them perished miserably.

Another time about the fourth Watch, early in the morning he fell upon several Casics, Noblemen and other Indians, who lookt upon themselves to be safe enough, (for they had their faith and security given, that none of them should receive any damage or injury) relying upon this, they left the Mountains their lurking places, without any suspition or fear, and returned to their Cities, but he seized on them all, and commanding them to extend their hands on the ground, cut them off with his own Sword, saying, that he punished them after this maner, because they would not inform him what Lord it was, that succeeded in that Kingdom.

The Inhabitants of one of these Provinces, perceiving that four or five of their Governours were sent to the other World in a fiery Vehicle or Chariot, being terrified therewith, took to the Mountains for Sanctuary, there being four or five thousand in number, as appears by good Evidence; and the aforesaid Captain sends a Tyrant, more cruel than any of the rest after them. The Spaniards ascend the Mountains by force (for the Indians were naked an unarm'd) Proclaiming Peace, if they would desist and lay down their Arms, which the Indians no sooner heard, but quitted their Childish Weapons; and this was no sooner done but this Sanguinary Spaniard sent some to possess themselves of the Fortifications, and they being secur'd, to attaque the Indians. Thus they, like Wolves and Lyons, did rush upon this flock of Sheep, and were so tired with slaughter, that they were forced to desist for a while and take breath, which done, the Captain commands them to fall to it again at the same bloody rate, and precipitate all that survived the Butchery, from the top of the Mountain, which was of a prodigious height; and that was perform'd accordingly. And the Witnesses farther declare upon Oath, that they saw the bodies of about seven hundred Indians falling from the Mount at one time, like a Cloud obscuring the Air, who were all broken to pieces.

This very Tyrant came once to the city Cota, where he surprized abundance of Men, together with fifteen or twenty Casics of the highest rank and quality, whom he cast to the Dogs to be torn Limb-meal in pieces, and cut off the Hands of several Men and Women, which being run through with a pole, were exposed to be viewed and gaz'd upon by the Indians, where you might see at once seventy pair of hands, transfixed with Poles; nor is it to be forgotten, that he cut off the Noses of many Women and Children.

The Witnesses farther depose, that the Cruelties and great Slaughters committed in the aforesaid new Kingdom of Granada, by this Captain, and other Tyrants, the Destroyers of Mankind, who accompany him, and have power still given them by him to exercise the same, are such and so hainous, that if his Majesty does not opportunely apply some remedy, for the redress and prevention of such mischiefs for the future, (since the Indians are daily slaughtered to accumulate and enrich themselves with Gold, which the Inhabitants have been so rob'd of, that they are now grown bare, for what they had, they have disposed to the Spaniards already) this Kingdom will soon decay and be made desolate, and consequently the Land being destitute of Indians, who should manure it, will lye fallow and incultivated.

And here is to be noted, how pestilential and inhumane the cruelty of these Tyrants hath been, and how violently exercised, when as in two or three years space, they were all slain, and the Country wholly desolate and deserted, as those that have been Eye-witnesses can testifie; they having acted like Merciless Men, not having the fear of God and the King before their Eyes, but by the instigation of the Devil; so that it may well be said and affirmed, not one Person will be left alive, unless his Majesty does retard, and put a stop to the full career of their Cruelties, which I am very apt to believe, for I have seen with these very eyes of mine, many Kingdoms laid waste and depopulated in a small time. There are other stately Provinces on the Confines of the New Kindgom of Granada, as Popayan and Cali, together with three or four more above five hundred miles in length, which they destroyed, in the same manner, as they have done other places, and laid them absolutely waste by the prementioned Slaughters, who were very Populous, and the Soil very Fruitful. They who came among us from those Regions report, that nothing can be more deplorable or worthy of pity and commiseration, then to behold such large and great Cities totally ruinated, and intombed in their own Ashes, and that in a City adorn'd with 1000 or 2000 Fabricks, there are hardly now to be seen 50 standing, the rest being utterly demolished, or consum'd and levelled to the ground by Fire and in some parts Regions of 100 miles in length, (containing spacious Cities) are found absolutely destroyed and consumed by Fire.

Finally many great Tyrants who came out of the Perusian Kingdoms by the Quitonians Travelled to the said new Kindgom of Granada and Popayan, and by Carthagena and the Urabae, they directed their course to Calisium, and several other Tyrants of Carthagena assault Quito, who joyn'd themselves in an intire Body and wholly depopulated and laid waste that Region for the space of 600 miles and upward, with the loss of a prodigious number of poor Souls; nor as yet do they treat the small remnant of so great and innocent a people with more humanity then formerly.

I desire therefore that the Readers who have or shall peruse these passages, would please seriously to consider whether or no, such Barbarous, Cruel and Inhumane Acts as these do not transcend and exceed all the impiety and tyrrany, which can enter into the thoughts or imagination of Man, and whether these Spaniards deserve not the name of Devils. For which of these two things is more eligible or desirable whether the Indians should be delivered up to the Devils themselves to be tormented or the Spaniards? That is still a question.

Nor can I here omit one piece of Villany, (whether it ought to be postpon'd or come behind the cruelty of Brute Animals, that I leave to decision). The Spaniards who are conversant among the Indians bred up curst Curs, who are so well instructed and taught that they at first sight, fly upon the Inhabitants tearing them limb by limb, and so presently devour them. Now let all persons whether Christians or not consider, if ever such a thing as this reacht the ears of any Man, they carry these Dogs with them as Companions where ever they go, and kill the fettered Indians in multitudes like Hogs for their Food;

thus sharing with them in the Butchery. Nay they frequently call one to the other, saying, lend me the fourth part of one of your Slaves to feed my Dogs, and when I kill one, I will repay you, as if they had only borrowed a quarter of a Hog or Sheep. Others, when they go a Hunting early in the morning, upon their return, if you ask them what sport had you to day at the Game? They will answer, enough, enough, for my Dogs have killed and worried 15 or 20 Indian Vassals. Now all these things are plainly prov'd upon those Inquisitions and Examinations made by one Tyrant against another. What I beseech you, can be more horrid or barbarous?

But I will desist from Writing any longer at this time, till some Messenger brings an account of greater and blacker Impieties (if greater can be committed) or else till we come to behold them again, as we have done for the space of forty two years with our own Eyes. I will only make this small addition to what I have said that the Spaniards, from the beginning of their first entrance upon America to this present day, were no more sollicitous of promoting the Preaching of the Gospel of Christ to these Nations, then if they had been Dogs or Beasts, but which is worst of all, they expressly prohibited their addresses to the Religious, laying many heavy Impositions upon them, dayly afflicting and persecuting them, that they might not have so much time and leasure at their own disposal, as to attend their Preaching and Divine Service; for they lookt upon that to be an impediment to their getting Gold, and raking up riches which their Avarice stimulated them so boundlessly to prosecute. Nor do they understand any more of a God, whether he be made of Wood, Brass or Clay, then they did above an hundred years ago, New Spain only exempted, which is a small part of America, and was visited and instructed by the Religious. Thus they did formely and still do perish without true Faith, or the knowledge and benefit of our Religious Sacraments.

I Frier Bartholomeas de las Casas or Casaus of the Order of St. Dominick, who through the mercy of God am Arriv'd at the Spanish Court, Cordially wishing the expulsion of Hell or these Hellish Acts out of the Indies; fearing least those Souls redeemed by the pretious Blood of Christ, should perish eternally, but heartily desiring that they may acknowledge their Creator and be saved; as also for the care and compassion that I ever had for my Native Countrey Castile, dreading least God should destroy it for the many sins committed by the Natives her Children, against Faith, Honour and their Neighbours: I have at length upon the request of some Persons of great Quality in this Court, who are fervently zealous of the Honour of God, and moved with pitty at the Calamities and Afflictions of their Neighbours (though I long since proposed it within my self, and resolved to accomplish it, but could not, being distracted with the avocations of multiplicity of constant Business and Employment, have leisure to effect it) I say I have at length finished this Treatise and Summary at Valencia, Decemb. 8. An. Dom. 1542, when they were arrived at the Height, and utmost Degree of executing Violences, Oppressions, Tyrany, Desolations, Torments, and Calamities in all the aforesaid Regions, Inhabited by the Spaniards (though they are more Cruel in some places than other) yet Mexico with its Confines were more favourably treated than the rest of the Provinces.

And indeed no Man durst openly and publickly do any injury to the Inhabitants; for there some Justice, (which is no where else in India) though very little is done and practiced; yet they are grievously opprest with intolerable Taxes. But I do really believe, and am fully perswaded that our Sovereign Lord Charles the Fifth, Emperour and King of Spain, our Lord and Prince, who begins to be sensible of the Wickedness and Treacheries, which have been, and still are committed against this Miserable Nation, and distressed Countries contrary to the Will and Pleasure of God, as well as His Majesties that he will in time, (for hitherto the Truth hath been concealed and kept from his Knowledge, with as great Craft, as Fraud and Malice) totally extirpate and root up all these Evils and Mischiefs, and apply such proper Medicines as may purge the Morbifick and peccant Humours in the Body Politick of this New World, committed to his Care and Government as a Lover and Promoter of Peace and

Tranquility. God preserve and bless him with Renown and a happy Life in his Imperial State, and prosper him in all his Attempts, that he may remedy the Distempers of the Christian Church, and Crown him at last with Eternal Felicity, Amen.

After I had published this Treatise, certain Laws and Constitutions, enacted by his Majesty then at Baraclona in the Month of December, An. Dom. 1542, promulgated and published the Year ensuing in the City of Madera, whereby it is provided, (as the present Necessities requir'd) that a period be put to such great Enormities and Sins, as were committed against God and our Neighbours, and tended to the utter Ruine and Perdition of this New World. These Laws were published by his Majesties Order, several Persons of highest Authority, Councellors, Learned, and Conscientious Men, being assembled together for that purpose, and many Debates made at Valedolid about this weighty Affair, at length by the unanimous Consent and Advice of all those who had committed their Opinions to Writing, they were made publick who traced more closely therein the Laws of Christ and Christianity, and were judged Persons pure, free from and innocent of that stain and blemish of depriving the Indians of their Treasures by Theft and Rapine, which Riches had contaminated and sullied the Hands, but much more the Souls of those who were enslav'd by those heaps of Wealth and Covetousness, now this obstinate and hot pursuit after Wealth was the Original of all those Evils committed without the least Remorse or Check of Conscience.

These Laws being thus promulgated, the Courtiers who promoted these Tyrants, took care that several Copies should be transcribed, (though they were extremely afflicted to see, that there was no farther hopes or means to promote the former Depredations and Extortions by the Tyranny aforesaid) and sent them to several Indian Provinces. They, who took upon them the Trouble and Care of Extirpating, and Oppressing by different ways of Cruelty, as they never observed any Method or Order, but behav'd themselves most inordinately and irregularly, having perused these Diplomata or

Constitutions, before the new made Judges, appointed to put them in Execution, could Arrive or be Landed, they by the assistance of those (as 'tis credibly rumour'd, nor is it repugnant to truth) who hitherto favour'd their Criminal and Violent Actions, knowing well that these Laws and Proclamations must necessarily take effect, began to grow mutinous, and rebel, and when the Judges were Landed, who were to Execute these Mandates, laying aside all manner of Love and Fear of God, were so audacious as to contemn and set at nought all the Reverence and Obedience due to their King, and so became Traytors, demeaning themselves like Blood-Thirsty Tyrants, destitute and void of all Humanity.

More particularly this appear'd in the Perusian Kingdoms, where An. Dom. 1542, they acted such Horrid and Stupendous Enormities, that the like were never known or heard in America, or throughout the whole World before that time: Nor were they only practised upon the Indians, who were mostly destroy'd, but upon themselves also, God permitting them by his just Judgement to be their own Executioners, and sheath their Swords in one anothers Bowels. In like manner the other parts of this New World being moved by the Example of these Rebels, refused to yield Obedience to those Laws. The rest pretending to petition his Majesty turn Rebellious themselves; for they would not voluntarily resign those Estates, Goods and Chattels they have already usurped, nor willingly manumit those Indians, who were doomed to be their Slaves, during Life; and where they restrain'd the Murdering Sword from doing Execution, they opprest them gradually with personal Vassalage, injust and intolerable Burthens; which his Majesty could not possibly hitherto avert or hinder, because they are all universally, some publickly and openly, others clancularly and secretly, so naturally addicted to Rob, Thieve and Steal; and thus under pretext of serving the King, they dishonour God, and defraud his Imperial Majesty.

Here the Author having finished the matter of Fact in this Compendious History, for Confirmation of what he has here written, quotes a tedious and imperfect Epistle (as he styles it) beginning and ending anonymous withal, containing the Cruelties committed by the Spaniards, the same in effect as our Author has prementioned, now in regard that I judge such reiterated Cruelties and repeated Barbarisms are Offensive to the Reader, he having sailed already too long, and too far in an Ocean of Innocent Indian blood: I have omitted all but Two or Three Stories not taken notice of by the Author. One of the Tyrants, (who followed the steps of John Ampudia, a notorious Villain) gave way to a grat Slaughter of Sheep the chief Food and Support of the Spaniards as well as Indians, permitting them to kill Two or Three Hundred at a time, only for their Brains, Fat, or Suet, whose Flesh was then altogether useless, and not fit to be eaten; but many Indians, the Spaniards Friends and Confederates followed them, desiring they might have the hearts to feed upon, whereupon they butchered a great many of them, for this only Reason, because they would not eat the other parts of the Body. Two of their gang in the Province of Peru kild Twenty Five Sheep, who were sold among the Spaniards for Twenty Five Crowns, merely to get the fat and brains out of them: Thus the frequent and extraordinary Slaughter of their Sheep above a Hundred Thousand Head of Cattel were destroy'd. And upon this Account the Region was reduced to great penury and want, and at length perished with Hunger. Nay the Province of Quito, which abounded with Corn beyond Expression, by such proceedings as these, was brought to that Extremity that a Sextarie or small Measure or Wheat was sold for Ten Crowns, and a Sheep at as dear a rate.

This Captain taking leave of Quito was followed by a poor Indianess with loud Cries and Clamours, begging and beseeching him not to carry away her Husband; for she had the charge of Three Children, and could not possibly supply them with Victuals, but they must inevitably dye with hunger, and though the Captain repulsed her with an angry brow at the first; yet she approacht him a second time with repeated Cries, saying, that her Children must perish for want of Food; but finding the Captain inexorable and altogether unmov'd with her Complaints, and her Husband not restor'd, through a piquant necessity wedded to despair; she cut off the Heads of her Children with sharp Stones, and so dispatcht them into the other World.

Then he proceeded farther to another City, and sent some Spaniards that very Night, to take the Indians of the City of Tulilicui, who next day brought with them above a Hundred Persons; some of which (whom he lookt upon to be able to carry burthens) he reserved for his own and his Soldiers service, and other were chain'd, and perished in their Fetters: but the little Infants he gave to the Casic of Tulilicui, abovesaid to be eaten up and devoured, whose skins are stuft with Ashes and hung up in his House to be seen at this very day. And in the close of this Letter he shuts up all with these words, 'tis here very remarkable and never to be forgotten, that this Tyrant (being not ignorant of the Mischiefs and Enormities executed by him) boastingly said of himself, They who shall travel in these Countreys Fifty years hence, and hear the things related of me, will have cause to say or declare, that never such a Tyrant as I am marched through these Regions, and committed the like Enormities.

Now not to quit the Stage without one Comical Scene or Action whereon such Cruelties have been lively personated, give me leave to acquaint you with a Comical piece of Grammatical Learning in a Reverend Religioso of these parts, sent thither to convert the West-Indies Pagans, which the Author mentions among his Reasons and Replications, and all these I pass by as immaterial to our purpose, many of them being repeated in the Narrative before.

The weight and burthen of initiating the Indians into the Christian Faith lay solely on the Spaniards at first; and therefore Joannes Colmenero in Santa Martha, a Fantastic, Ignorant, and Foppish Fellow, was under Examination before us (and he had one of the most spatious Cities committed to his Charge as well as the Care and Cure of the Souls of the Inhabitants) whether he understood how to fortifie himself with the sign of the Cross against the Wicked and Impious, and being interrogated what he taught, and how he instructed the Indians, whose Souls were intrusted to his Care and Conduct; he return'd this Answer, That if he damn'd them to the Devil and Furies of Hell, it was sufficient to retrieve them, if he pronounced these Words, Per Signin Sanctin Cruces. A Fellow fitter to be a Hogherd than a Shepherd of Souls.

This Deep, Bloody American Tragedy is now concluded, and my Pen choakt up with Indian Blood and Gore. I have no more to say, but pronounce the Epilogue made by the Author, and leave the Reader to judge whether it deserves a Plaudite.

The Spaniards first set Sail to America, not for the Honour of God, or as Persons moved and merited thereunto by servent Zeal to the True Faith, nor to promote the Salvation of their Neighbours, nor to serve the King, as they falsely boast and pretend to do, but in truth, only stimulated and goaded on by insatiable Avarice and Ambition, that they might for ever Domineer, Command, and Tyrannize over the West- Indians, whose Kingdoms they hoped to divide and distribute among themselves. Which to deal candidly in no more or less intentionally, than by all these indirect wayes to disappoint and expel the Kings of Castile out of those Dominions and Territories, that they themselves having usurped the Supreme and Regal Empire, might first challenge it as their Right, and then possess and enjoy it.

Made in the USA
San Bernardino, CA
15 May 2020